NOW I SEA

CW01629480

WHAT READERS ARE SAYING

In a world full of turmoil, I savored every insightful chapter of Jenny L. Cote's *Now I Sea.* Right from the start, it felt like a refreshing ocean breeze, soothing my soul, and bringing me into harmony with God.

—*Libby McNamee, Author & Speaker*

Hop aboard for a grand adventure in Jenny L. Cote's updated *Now I Sea.* Jenny's words will inspire, challenge, thrill, and comfort you. The Great Admiral whispered them to her many years ago. In His mercy, she has since lived them as He carved them into her heart. Enjoy learning the story behind the story, *behind* the story. Soak in the love of your heavenly Father and take in all the insights He meant specifically for you.

—*Claire Roberts Foltz, Author & Teacher*

Jenny has written of how a person can find adventure and fulfillment in both the natural and the spiritual realms, making life exciting and blessed.

—*Dr. Paul Mims*

Jenny L. Cote's *Now I Sea* seamlessly combines nautical journeys with those of faith, and she includes just the right touch of adventure and accessibility. Though she's a bestselling YA author, this inspiring book of faith is enlightening for readers of all ages!

—*Bridget Creech, Bahamas Children's Mission*

I have long found refuge at the beach, especially after suffering life's storms. There is something about standing there with the smell of salty air, the sound of the waves hitting the shore, and the sight of the expansive ocean which brings assurance of the fact that the One who created this sacred place can bring us salvage after life's storms. Jenny's use of coastal analogies and the attributes of God will embolden any reader to set sail in their journey on sails of grace.

—*Beth Cuvelier, Attorney & Teacher*

AMAZON FIVE STAR REVIEWS FROM THE 2003 EDITION

So well done! Relevant and poignant.

—Lance

Whether you love the sea, or, like me, prefer the mountains, this book is a refreshingly personal approach to faith in life.

—Monica

Jenny's book helps us navigate the spiritual seas we all are on and know that God is truly in control.

—Leland

My husband is the sailor, not I. But I was neither intimidated nor bored by this book. Mrs. Cote's passionate relationship with God and her love of the sea drew me in. Each chapter not only taught me but fed me food for thought. The author's examples of being aware of and comfortable with God are easy to share with others. This is the kind of book I can go back to again and again both as a devotional and just for pleasure. I'm looking forward to more books by this new author.

—Barbara

This book has wonderful biblical insight around interesting life events of the author. Jenny L. Cote is an excellent writer—highly recommend ALL her books!

—Diana (Germany)

NOW I SEA

Spiritual Life Lessons from the Sea

JENNY L. COTE

Jenny L. Cote

Now I Sea: Spiritual Life Lessons from the Sea

Copyright © 2024 by Jenny L. Cote.

Published by Jenny L. Cote Publications.

All rights reserved. Except for brief quotations in printed reviews, no part of this book may be reproduced, stored in a retrieval system, or transmitted in any form or by any means (printed, written, photocopied, visual electronic, audio, or otherwise) without prior permission from the author.

Printed Edition: ISBN: 979-8-89217-226-4
ePUB Edition: ISBN: 979-8-89217-225-7

Scripture quotations marked "NJKV" are taken from the New King James Version. Copyright © 1982 by Thomas Nelson, Inc. Used by permission. All rights reserved.

Scripture quotations marked "ESV" are taken from The Holy Bible, English Standard Version. Copyright © 2000, 2001 by Crossway Bibles, a division of Good News Publishers. Used by permission. All rights reserved.

Scripture quotations marked (NIV) are taken from the HOLY BIBLE, NEW INTERNATIONAL VERSION ®. NIV ®. Copyright © 1973, 1978, 1984 by International Bible Society. Used by permission of Zondervan. All rights reserved.

Scripture quotations marked (NLT) are taken from the Holy Bible. New Living Translation copyright © 1996, 2004, 2007 by Tyndale House Publishers, Inc. Used by permission. All rights reserved.

Scripture quotations marked (KJV) are taken from the King James Version (Authorized Version), which is in the public domain.

Cover by Rob Moffitt, Chicago, Illinois.
Interior design by Katherine Lloyd, theDESKonline.com.
Interior images from Canva, Shutterstock, and Jenny L. Cote.
Editing by Richard Cairnes, Walworth, Wisconsin.

Printed in United States of America.

For my parents—
who trained me up in the way I should go,
with a believer's heart for God
and a sailor's passion for the sea.

God called the dry ground "land,"
and the gathered waters he called "seas."
And God saw that it was good.
—Genesis 1:10, NIV

CONTENTS

PART FOUR:
GOING ASHORE

PART FIVE:
NOW I SEA EVEN MORE

PART SIX:
BACK IN PORT

FOREWORD

I ask for your forgiveness in advance if, for any reason, I am found guilty of automatically assuming that you, too, have a love for the sea and everything it offers, as my wife, Lisa, and I do. In her masterfully written work, *Now I Sea*, author Jenny L. Cote has managed to pen a colorful, thought-provoking, and meaningful journey. She leads the reader through the delights of life—those moments when all is clear and smooth, and the sun is shining as you feel the wind in your sails. And with equal relevance, Jenny reminds us that there is also a course we must sail that draws us ever closer to the Great Navigator of life Himself, Jesus Christ, as He helms the vessel that bears your name. It's of great comfort to experience the fact that when the skies darken and storms bring their tribulations, He who is mighty to save will bring you safely into His haven of rest.

I speak for Lisa and myself when I say that from one chapter to the next, *Now I Sea* challenged us to become more childlike in our faith and have greater trust in our God. The impact of *Now I Sea* has helped us to see things from a much higher vantage point regarding the goodness and sweetness of God and His love for us in everyday life. Having been born in San Diego, California, and later moving to Orange County, I thought everything about the sea and its benefits were just part of life. As kids, we would spend our summers, year after year, in and out of the water. We couldn't get enough of what God had made for us to experience! Looking back over my life, much has changed as age and time will do that to all of us, but for some reason, my family and I must get to the shore for no other reason than to see the water. Every time we do, it's a reunion of memories and great significance. In fact, it was at the shore that the Lord brought to me my wife, who has traveled alongside me for more than forty-five years. Sea? Good things await there!

Perhaps you enjoy just sitting on the shore listening to the rhythm of the waves or watching a distant sailboat patiently, perfectly continuing its course. Or maybe you're one for the high seas and the thrill of it all. No matter your preference, we desire that you receive as much insight from Jenny's practical applications as Lisa and I have. There is so much here for the meditation of your heart and mind to help you discover that Jesus is the anchor you need.

We believe that as you read *Now I Sea*, you will find yourself yielding to the command of God's creation—to slow down and take in the beauties and the tranquilities that God has woven into the fabric of His creation for your pure enjoyment and to His great praise.

Awaiting His Return,
Jack Hibbs
Pastor, Calvary Chapel Chino Hills, CA

PROLOGUE

MUCH TO SEA

The French philosopher Pascal once said that inside each of us is a God-shaped void. Other than God Himself, nothing can bring peace and true lifelong happiness. I believe this to be true: God has filled my own emptiness as nothing else can . . . as only He could.

And yet, although I know my soul is secure—now and forever—sometimes my relationship with God gets rough around the edges due to my less-than-perfect behavior. Keeping that God-shaped puzzle piece in mint condition is an everyday practice, a lifelong process. I fall and must get back up. I soar to spiritual heights, then must come back down. Spiritual growth is never complete. And I consider that a blessing.

I'd like to add to the metaphor of the God-shaped void. For while it's true that God is the only One who can complete the puzzle of our true selves, He doesn't presume to meet the needs of vastly different people all in the same way. Rather, He tailor-makes additional experiences and attributes that perfectly meet each void-holder. Spiritual growth happens in a multitude of ways as God provides perfect avenues for each soul.

Some people experience growth through intellectual discovery, others through worship or service, and others still through nature, just to name a few. I tend to grow on several planes but feel the greatest growth spurts as I get to know God better through nature. In part this is because of the meaningful parallels I see between God's divine nature and the nature He created. But mostly it has to do with the fact that in nature I escape the distractions that keep me from hearing God as I should in my everyday world. You see, my void has sails attached to it, and I feel God's presence most strongly when my senses fill with coastal sights, sounds, and breezes.

I believe God speaks to people through the human experience via physical places on Earth that touch the soul in unusual ways. For some it might be a mountaintop. For others, it might be an expansive ranch with distant horizons. For others still, a lake, a forest, a desert, or a snow-covered land—any of God's natural landscapes—can serve as a soul-connection where we experience God's clear presence amid our joys and our struggles. Just as God miraculously created everyone with a totally unique personality, voice, and physical appearance, I think He also gave us as a gift a special place on Earth to meet Him in a visual, tangible way. It's a place where God says, "Hey, meet me there as soon as you can so we can share some wonderful things. I've got so much to tell you and to show you."

My soul-connection place is the coast. Any coast will do if the water is salty, the sand is plentiful, and sailboats are nearby. I can tell when the wind has left my sails and I need God to make them full. Saltwater runs deep in my veins, and my soul aches when I am away from it for too long. My coast love was ingrained in me from the beginning, having grown up on the Virginia coast as a sailor on Chesapeake Bay. I now live inland, but God in His loving grace has allowed the boundary lines to fall in pleasant places for me. Our house overlooks a river and I love to go sit on rocks surrounded by racing currents to enjoy its beauty. This fresh water is wonderful, and I am ever thankful for such a blessing—but for me, it's not the same without the vast horizon, without the salt.

PROLOGUE: MUCH TO SEA

I have often wondered why God would instill in me such a love for the sea yet take me away from it. Perhaps He knew that my love and desire to be there would grow. Maybe He wanted to reserve a special place for my deep encounters with Him so I would not become complacent about the soul-connection landscape in my heart. Rather, God *must* have known that I would come running back into His presence with tears of joy to be there again . . . because that is exactly what happens.

As I approach the coast on every return trip, I gasp for that first breath of salt air. I strain my ears for that first sound of crashing waves . . . or of noisily clanging mast halyards. My internal halyards clang, and my sails begin to fill almost immediately. A wonderful cruise begins, and I start humming a favorite Jimmy Buffett tune as I grin from ear to ear.

God leaves His footprints in the sand of every life experience and delightfully shows me where He does so on these coastal excursions. With each footprint found comes a new insight into who God really is, and with each insight comes a rush of discovery and joy. I find His footprints in the spiritual sand of my heart as well as in the physical sand under my feet.

This book is the log of a cruise along many coasts with God at the helm. It is a navigation through seas of insight, via navigation through various seas of water and beaches around the world. I welcome you to come along with me so I can share with you points of interest along the way. Sometimes our discoveries will be metaphorical, sometimes physically literal as we explore the wonders of the sea and the coast as they relate to the human experience. We'll watch God walk along the beaches of birth and death, family and friendships, hopes and dreams, exploration and adventure, life challenges and storms, war and pain, and healing and restoration. So, come along with me as we skip along the surface to enjoy the light-hearted, crystal blue seas of the soul and plunge into deep waters to reach the rarely touched depths of the soul. Time to cast off. Conditions are favorable—the winds are perfect, the tides are with us, and the sun is warm and inviting. Whether you are a fellow sailor or a confirmed landlubber, I hope that at the end of our cruise you will be able to also say, "Oh, hey, God—*now* I sea!"

PART ONE

CASTING OFF

"It is very difficult to say where a voyage begins.
First of course there must be a dream,
a longing for out-of-the-way places."
—Peter Hamilton[1]

The anchor heaves, the ship swings free,
The sails swell full. To sea, to sea!

—Thomas Lovell Beddoes[1]

Chapter 1

SAILBOAT DREAMS

There is much to learn from the sea and from life in general aboard a boat. When you climb aboard a sailboat, especially for an extended trip, you enter a different world. The "roughing it" way of living, the places you go, the people you meet, the nature you encounter—all are privileges I hold dear.

One chapter cannot contain all there is to glean from the world of sailing. One book cannot do so. But my job as cruise director is not to show you everything there is to see, but to illuminate points of interest along the way—to share with you a few God-inspired insights on this aspect of the sea. So, I would like to guide you over a handful of waters in the vast bay of a sailor's mind and heart.

Sailing is not something that begins with a thought. It begins with a dream. The thoughts will come—plenty of them—but a seed of desire to be one with the sea begins with a dream.

A Dream Is Born

When I was five years old, my father caught a serious bug—a sailboat bug. We were living in Norfolk, Virginia, at the time, and our natural surroundings were filled with nautical imagery. Norfolk sits at the lower end of Chesapeake Bay and is home to sailors from around the world. Our house was across the street from the Lafayette River, which I could see from my corner bedroom window. We crossed that river daily on our way to various ordinary destinations, and glimpsed white sails gliding gracefully down the Lafayette to reach Chesapeake Bay. When you are exposed to such beauty every day, it's hard not to get enthralled with the idea of hopping on one of those sailboats to see what it's like.

In 1969, my then-31-year-old dad read an article in *National Geographic* magazine about a 16-year-old boy, Robin Lee Graham, and his adventure of sailing solo around the world in his 23-foot sailboat, *Dove.* From that incredible inspiration, my dad began to dream about entering this new world of sailing. Having grown up on a South Georgia farm, sailing was indeed a new world. So, just as anyone sets out to make a dream reality, he began with something small. "Do not despise these small beginnings, for the LORD rejoices to see the work begin" (Zechariah 4:10, NLT).

Dad purchased a mighty vessel: a nine-foot catboat with a single sail and a centerboard. He launched the no-named tub into the Lafayette River with great aspirations of salty adventure. Salty was right! My mom was on the shore commenting to a friend about how safe the little boat was, just as it capsized. After several unsuccessful tacks, with sails more in the water than in the air, he started to get the hang of it. Mrs. Vogan, my piano teacher who lived around the corner, kept our little boat behind her house on the river. Over the course of a year, dad developed sea legs and even greater sailboat dreams.

Sea Bird Beginnings

Oh, how dreams do grow!

Selling our nine-foot tub, Dad then bought a 1947 wooden, 36-foot Atkins' design cutter rig replete with crow's nest. Not only was this sailboat four times larger, but she also had a name: *Sea Bird.* We didn't name her but decided to let our first "real" sailboat keep the name to which she was already attached. Learning the finer points of boat naming would come later. We also moved up in our mooring standards, from my piano teacher's backyard dock to a real marina. It was at Willoughby Bay Marina in Norfolk that we became indoctrinated in sailboat ownership. The *Sea Bird* joined the ranks of those tall masts reaching skyward while tied to their secure docks.

From that day on, I have loved the sights and sounds of marinas. I'm captivated by row upon row of sailboats with creaking boat lines and clanging mast halyards. One thing I discovered early on at Willoughby Bay was splinters—you can't run far down a wooden dock without picking up a few. But shoes just aren't as fun when you're in a hurry to net a crab hanging on a dock piling!

It was also with the *Sea Bird* that *my* sailing aspirations began. I was born with a *carpe diem* spirit of adventure, so the freedom of sailing naturally appealed to me. At the age of six, I climbed to the top of the crow's nest to see what I could see. It took my mom a while to find me, and to recover once she did. I think she's the one who brought to my attention the fact that I was up so high, and she did so rather *loudly.* The view of the horizon was great, but the view down the mast was scary. I froze.

Sailing Life, Lesson 1. *Never climb to the top until you are prepared to come down.* Enthusiasm and eagerness are good things, but they can lead you into situations for which you are not prepared if you don't fully understand the heights involved. How easy it is to forget the view and freeze when reality sets in.

Dad climbed up to me, speaking gentle words of calming assurance. He told me exactly what to do to get down. Not only did he tell me how to climb down backward, but he also surrounded me with his arms to make sure I wouldn't fall. That is exactly how our heavenly Father reacts when we freeze after getting into precarious situations. He calmly climbs to where we are stuck and gently tells us exactly what to do. Then He lovingly protects us while we get back down on more solid footing.

Well, I wasn't the only one who got stuck—the *Sea Bird* herself was, too. There's this little thing you need to remember when underway. A sailboat has a keel (on the underside, to help keep it upright), and shallow water will stop you. On a short cruise to Coinjock, North Carolina, we ran aground. No attempts at reversing the engine would release us. This time it was the U.S. Coast Guard who came to the rescue, pulling us from the shoal to deeper water. I cannot tell you how proud *that* made us feel. We may as well have had a flag flying off the crow's nest: *Caution! Novice Sailors Aboard!* Nothing like a good dose of humility.

Sailing Life, Lesson 2. *Know your limitations.* That old keel under the *Sea Bird* taught us this important life lesson. In the water, and in life, one must pay attention to the depths as well as the heights. Remember what's below the waterline. Know how deep the water is through which you are navigating.

But most importantly, know that God will always be there to help you when you make mistakes. Mistakes are a part of living and discovery. God knows that's how we novice life-livers learn best. He allows us to make mistakes without His intervention, in order for us to grow. When we call for help, He will always come. He will never let us fall, nor will He ever let us remain stuck. Why? Because not only does He love us as His children, but He also loves us as the wonderful dreamers He made us to be.

So, I look forward to someday cruising the Virgin Islands on the West Sail 42 I've always wanted.

Sailing Life, Lesson 3. Hey, a sailor can *dream*, can't she?

With ships the sea was sprinkled far and nigh,
Like stars in heaven, and joyously it showed;
Some lying fast at anchor in the road,
Some veering up and down, one knew not why.
A goodly vessel did I then espy
Come like a giant from a haven broad;
And lustily along the bay she strode,
Her tackling rich, and of apparel high.
The ship was nought to me, nor I to her,
Yet I pursued her with a lover's look;
This ship to all the rest did I prefer:
When will she turn, and whither? She will brook
No tarrying; where She comes the winds must stir:
On went She, and due north her journey took.

—William Wordsworth[1]

Chapter 2

THE LOVE BOAT

The funny thing about a sailboat is that with every additional foot in length comes a proportionate increase in the amount of time and money needed to care for it. Seeing as how we didn't have much of either, after two years of owning the *Sea Bird,* we decided to sell her and decrease the size of the sailboat, but not the size of the dream.

What we did was continue to search for the perfect boat love of our lives. Just as with finding the love of your life in a person, sometimes it takes going through a few prospects along the way. The time invested in those prospects is never wasted. It helps to crystallize more of what it is you really want in the love of your life.

Homemade Love

Sometimes love prospects aren't very exciting or fancy. Sometimes they just are nice and . . . like homemade. That's literally what our next sailboat was—homemade. Dad met a man serving in the Coast Guard who was looking to sell his 21-foot Luger sailboat kit, which was 75% complete. It seemed like a great idea to Dad, so he bought the kit and finished it in our backyard. We named this boat the *Joe-Lynne,* after my brother and me.

Once we launched her into the water, we decided to take her on short weekend trips. We never went farther than forty miles. That's all we could handle! Since we couldn't afford cushions, we slept on quilts on top of wooden planks. Mom cooked on a two-burner stove while sitting on a "chair" (which was also the porta-potty). Her refrigerator was a large cooler. And of course, we couldn't stand up straight in the boat because there wasn't enough headroom.

Ah, the luxurious life of sailing.

After a year of this flirting, which we knew would never amount to anything, we sold the *Joe-Lynne.* Although we were able to create some warm memories, she just wasn't what we wanted. It was time to move on in our search for true boat love.

Boat Show Bliss

After selling the *Joe-Lynne*, we ventured to the 1974 boat show in Hampton Roads, Virginia. Our mouths watered at all the brand-new boats we saw. New . . . what a concept! Wow, cushions, the high life! Our eyes finally settled on a 23-foot Coronado, and we bought her.

We decided to name this boat *Agape,* which means supreme love, or God's love. We were so grateful to God for allowing us to become sailors and proud owners of this fine vessel that we wanted to express our gratitude in a tangible way. Although we couldn't stand up straight inside *Agape* either, we had much more space and much more comfort. So, we took her on a real cruise. We sailed over three hundred miles from Norfolk to Wilmington, North Carolina. Although we had a wonderful time, I remember two especially unpleasant events on this trip.

I became extremely sick with a high fever. Have you ever had a fever . . . on a boat with no air conditioning . . . in August? It was not fun, but what a thing to understand about boat life. You might be able to sail away from it all, but you still take your body with you, and you can still get sick. So *Agape* was with me in sickness and in health.

The other unpleasant memory aboard *Agape* began on one especially hot day when Joe and I decided we wanted to get pulled behind the boat in the water to cool off. We donned lifejackets and jumped over, holding on to a rope while Dad took pictures of us having fun. It felt great! But the pleasant memory would not last long.

That night we docked in Elizabeth City, North Carolina, and spent a luxurious evening inside an air-conditioned restaurant and theater. There was this new movie out . . . *Jaws*. What a fine, heartwarming, hope-filled plot. Not only did I scream my 10-year-old lungs out; not only was I ruined for life in thinking about *Jaws* whenever I now step foot in the ocean; my stomach sank when I thought about what we had done that afternoon. Joe and I had been shark bait! And when we got those pictures developed, way back behind us in the water there is something that looks like a fin.

Not all the memories about *Agape* were unpleasant. Those bad moments just exist amid happy times. That's part of having a realistic love life. We were able to enjoy living aboard a boat for an extended period. We saw and experienced so many wonderful things. *Agape* was a more serious relationship, but for the long haul, she just wasn't the one. She sailed well, but we wanted more in a boat. So, after two years, we moved on.

The Love Boat Comes In

We realized that to truly have the boat love of our lives, it was going to require a greater commitment. As with traditional wedding vows, this was not something to be entered into lightly, but advisedly, soberly, and in the fear of God! It was important to my parents that this be a family decision. This was going to be a big investment requiring a leap of faith because we lived on a modest income. We wanted the choice to be based on a family sport that everyone could enjoy—one that two young children could be happy with as we grew and spent lots of time together.

So, one August afternoon in 1976, our family drove over to Bluewater Yachts in Hampton, Virginia. There, sitting in the boat yard, was the love boat we had been searching for. She was a Cal 2-29 sailboat, white with hunter green stripes. Her shiny fiberglass hull glistened in the sun.

She had standing room, a beautiful teakwood interior, a working head (toilet), a shower, a galley (kitchen) with a big icebox, a diesel inboard engine . . . and soft cushions to just die for! It was love at first sight. There was something about this boat that just *felt* right. So, we signed the papers and committed ourselves to ten years of wedded monthly payments . . . for richer or poorer . . . 'til debt us do part.

But what to name her? After throwing around a few ideas, we all came to the same conclusion. We were just too attached to *Agape*. The people who had bought our first *Agape* changed the name of that boat, so we felt as though we should reclaim it for our own once again.

Our true love boat had finally come in. *Agape* was to become not just a family sporting vessel, but also a family *member*. Over the years we sailed *Agape* all over Chesapeake Bay and all down the Eastern seaboard to the Florida Keys. We even had her on an inland lake for 10 years. Times have been wonderful, but occasionally hard, especially during the college years when money was tight. But God always took care of us, and we held on to our love boat.

Never-ending Honeymoon

I sit here on *Agape* in August 2000, 24 years later, and am filled with as much joy and love for this boat as on the day we bought her. *Agape* has been our traveling companion, protector in storms, adventure guide, and constant giver of happy memories. Having *Agape* for our own has required sacrifice and commitment. But she has truly lived up to her name—supreme love.

We search in this life for a human lifelong love, a connection that I hope you have found or will find in your life. But our souls search for a love that is even deeper. God's love—Agape—is the love that is *truly* supreme. It is what we long for. Agape is sacrificial of its own accord, and it is committed to waiting for you until you find it. It is a protector in storms, companion for the journey, comforter in unpleasant times, and joyful giver of happy memories. Pursue *this* love until you find it. You will know the minute you see it that *this* is the love you've always wanted. This is the love you've been searching for. Nothing else will satisfy—or even come close. Agape is the love that will be with you always . . . a never-ending honeymoon through your lifetime and beyond.

Yet still, even now, my spirit within me
Drives me seaward to sail the deep,
To ride the long swell of the salt sea-wave.
Never a day but my heart's desire
Would launch me forth on the long sea-path,
Fain of far harbors and foreign shores.
Yet lives no man so lordly of mood,
So eager in giving, so ardent in youth,
So bold in his deeds, or so dear to his lord,
Who is free from dread in his far sea-travel,
Or fear of God's purpose and plan for his fate.

—Anonymous

Chapter 3

DAUGHTER OF A DAUGHTER OF A SAILOR

I love to sing along to Jimmy Buffett's song *Son of a Son of a Sailor* that talks about sailing forefathers of old. I can picture tall ships filled with salty crews out on the blue water sailing to foreign ports. It's too bad that "daughter of a daughter of a sailor" just doesn't flow as well because I'd love to sing this song that way. Why? Because that's exactly what I am—literally—in name. To help you understand what I mean, let me tell you a story that goes way back in time.

What's in a Name?

It's May 29, 1719, in Ittlingen, Germany. Maria Catharina is in labor, experiencing the pain of childbirth as women have done since time began. Her husband Andreas wipes the sweat from her brow as she tries to capture enough breath for the next contraction. There is pain in Andreas's eyes as he sees the pain in the eyes of his beloved wife. "Hold on, Maria. A little while longer," he gently whispers as he holds tightly to her hand.

At long last, a baby boy is born. The tender cries of protest from one entering this new, cold, confusing world fill the house. Tender tears from loving parents join those of the baby as this new life begins. Andreas looks at Maria, who softly holds the baby close in her arms, quieting the protesting little one. She looks back at her husband and says, "He is a fine son and will make us so happy. What name should we give to him?"

Andreas takes the baby in his arms and stares intently at the small, round, red face. "Why, Dietrich. That shall be his name. Dietrich Sailer."

Soon it is time to take Dietrich to their Lutheran church for baptism. The minister joins with the parents in this symbolic ceremony of birth in

Christ. Following tradition, the child is given yet another name, the name of a nobleman, which is Pleickerd.

Pleickerd Dietrich Sailer grows and becomes an apprentice of the village shepherd. In 1734, this 15-year-old boy is confirmed in the church. On his confirmation record for his occupation is written "in the service of the shepherd."

Although Dietrich is happy with his home and family, he hears a call in his heart leading him on to a new life. It is the call of the sea. It is the call of a new world—America. So much is happening over there! Colonies are forming; riches await all who land on her golden shores. Everything is new and exciting, and any thoughts of not experiencing America are more than Dietrich can bear.

One night, Dietrich approaches Andreas and Maria. "Father, Mother . . . I love you dearly. I am grateful for all you have taught me, and for all you have given me. I thank you for the unconditional love you have always shown me. I am proud to be your son. But I am twenty-two years old now. It is time for me to chart my own course—and I wish to go to America. I know, I know . . . I am leaving you and this homeland, but I must go see this new world. I must answer this longing in my heart. I know that by going I won't live up to our family tradition . . . but I just must . . . go."

With tears in his eyes, Andreas—wisely this time—does not try to silence Dietrich's proclamation, for he knows . . . and he understands. Andreas looks at Maria and knows her heart is breaking, but he knows that he must give Dietrich his blessing.

"Dietrich, your mother and I would love nothing more than for you to stay here with us forever. You have been our source of pride and joy since the day you were born. But our love for you must remain true to doing what parents must sometimes painfully do, to let you go. For—although you did not know it—you *are* living up to your family name and tradition. You are a Sailer. Our family name came from our ancestors long before us. They were rope-makers, and it is from our name that the word 'sailor' was born.

"You are following a call in your heart that was imprinted on your soul by your forefathers. The call of the sea is part of who we are as Sailers.

The sea is in our veins. You must go follow your heart's call. You have our blessing."

As they did more than two decades before, tender cries fill this humble home as father, mother, and son embrace.

With adrenaline coursing through his sea-filled veins, Dietrich makes his plans. Since he does not have enough money for passage to America, he sells himself as an indentured servant to the captain of a snow ship named *Two Sisters.* On a brisk day in 1741, Pleickerd Dietrich Sailer embarks on the journey of a lifetime. This Sailer becomes a sailor indeed.

On the voyage Dietrich meets the daughter of the captain: Elizabeth. She will be the love of his life. He vows to marry her but must wait until she is old enough to marry and until he is released from indenture. The captain sells Dietrich to a merchant in the colony of Pennsylvania.

After several years Dietrich and Elizabeth marry and start an entire new family of Sailers in America. They have a son, Jacob. Jacob has a son, Burgess. Burgess has a daughter, Nancy. Nancy has a son, Burgis. Burgis has a daughter, Debbie. Debbie has a son, Bryant. Bryant has a daughter, Janice. Janice marries a soon-to-be sailor Paul, and they have a daughter: Jenny. Jenny is raised to know the goodness of God and the wonder of the sea. She grows to womanhood, falls in love, marries a Georgia man, and takes his name: *Cote,* which in French means, "coast."

So here I am, daughter of a daughter of a Sailer *and* a sailor . . . and a mate of the coast. What's in a name? Quite a lot, I'd say.

When I first learned of my ancestor Dietrich, I became intrigued with the origin of my name. How uncanny that I am not just a sailor by experience, but I am a sailor by *name.* It was the occupation of my forefathers that inspired the name sailor—that's just about too much serendipity for me to handle. But I soon became intrigued with an even greater serendipity than that of my ancestor's name. I was struck by the imagery woven throughout Dietrich's story that mirrors the story of a child born into Christ.

A Heritage of Nobility

Dietrich experienced a physical birth, as we all do. But when he was baptized, he was symbolically born as a child of God. He was given a new name, Pleickerd, which was one of nobility. When we are born as children of God, we too, are given a new name that is one of nobility. We who accept Christ in our hearts become children of the King and are blessed with the noble family name—*Christian.*

Dietrich was raised in a Christian home of Sailers but worked in the fields of a shepherd. How beautiful that his confirmation read "in the service of the shepherd." Not only was Dietrich a literal servant of the village shepherd, but also, as a Christian, he was in the service of the Good Shepherd. He allowed the Shepherd to lead him throughout his life. And I'm sure that the call of the sea in Dietrich's heart was placed there by Christ the Shepherd.

The Shepherd knew the plans He had for Dietrich, plans not to harm him, but to prosper him, to give him hope and a future (Jeremiah 29:11). So, He also placed a call in Dietrich's heart to follow Him wherever He might lead so the plan could unfold.

Prosper him, He did. Dietrich and Elizabeth were richly blessed and gave birth to many children. Many of those children chose to carry on the family tradition, receiving the name of nobility, receiving confirmation of their personal faith, and serving the Shepherd. And some of those children's children even continued the family tradition of being a sailor.

Hmmm, I am of heavenly nobility, in the service of the Shepherd, and am living the life of a sailor—not a bad heritage, huh? All because of a Sailer born in 1719, and a Carpenter born in Bethlehem around 2 BC.

Thank you, my sixth great-grandfather Dietrich, for my rich family heritage on Earth. And thank you, my heavenly Father, for my rich spiritual heritage. I thank you that the sea's in my veins, that my tradition remains.

I hope you are blessed with the knowledge of your family history as well. I had a genealogy-researching uncle named Willie, who discovered Dietrich's story, and even read his actual baptism and confirmation entries at the Lutheran Church in Germany. I'm so thankful for Willie's discovery. What a blessing to know the story that culminates in the miracle of one's own life! But even if you don't know your family heritage of long past on Earth, I'm here to tell you that you have a rich family heritage in Heaven. It is a tremendous story . . . culminating in *you.*

Your Rich Heritage

Before the earth was formed, God knew you. He decided the century and the country in which you would be born. He heard your cries of protest as you entered this new, cold, confusing world. And He knew that as you grew, your world would become even more cold and confusing because of the sin in which it was engulfed. He knew that there was a jailer—death—that wanted to claim you for his own.

So, God had a plan, a plan to put you out of harm's way. It was a plan to prosper you with new life. It was a plan to give you hope and a future. It was a plan to keep you one step ahead of the jailer.

God loved you so much as His child that He allowed His Son—your big Brother—to come into this world long before you. Jesus came as the Shepherd to save those who were lost. He came with His powerful love and grace to make this world warm amid the coldness. And He died and rose again so you could claim the birthright of nobility for your own. Jesus wanted to take you back to a new world we call Heaven but knew you didn't have enough for the passage. So, He paid it for you by becoming indentured to sin and death for a short time—three days. Having been released from indenture, He wants to bring you into His family. He wants you to share in the family business—in the service of the Shepherd.

This is the rich heritage that is yours to claim. Have you adopted the name of nobility? Have you accepted the free passage to take your spirit to a wonderful, new world when it is time to leave this place and just . . . go? If not, claim your heritage. Change your name and get on board. Let God take you on the sail of your life—and allow Him to deliver you to the only new world that *really* has "gold-paved streets." You have a huge family waiting for you—don't miss the reunion.

It's going to be a son-of-a-gun of a chorus!

The Lord's time is like the time of the tide, which no human power can either accelerate or retard. Though it tarry, wait for it.

—John Newton

After waiting another seven days, Noah released the dove again. He waited another seven days and then released the dove again. This time it did not come back.

—Genesis 8:10,12, NLT

But if we look forward to something we don't yet have, we must wait patiently and confidently.

—Romans 8:25, NLT

Chapter 4

WAIT AND SEA

The Waiting Game

I just couldn't *wait* to get to the beach! Anticipating a long week of fun in the sun with my family and friends, spring break couldn't get here fast enough. But eventually it arrived, and off we were to St. George Island, Florida.

My husband Casey wasn't feeling well but was too busy to go to the doctor before we left. So, on our first night at the beach, he woke me at 3:00 a.m. with a 103-degree fever and said he had to get to the hospital. He was in agony with a painful sinus infection. I groggily got up, threw on some sweats and drove Casey to the Apalachicola hospital, which was twenty-five minutes away . . . concerned . . . but fuming. *Why did he* wait *so long to go to the doctor? If he had just gone before we left Atlanta, he'd feel good now, and I'd be snug in bed.* The doctor gave him a shot, but Casey would need antibiotics in the morning. Of course, there isn't a pharmacy on St. George, so after we got back on the island, I would have to *wait* for the drugstore to open . . . back over in Apalachicola.

We got home at 5:30 a.m., and I crashed on the couch after putting Casey to bed. The laughter of kids woke me up at 7:00 a.m. Plus, it was daylight savings time. ARRRGG! No use trying to sleep anymore. I called to see when the drugstore would open, and the recording said 9:00 a.m. Wishing I had an IV to pump coffee into my veins, I drank a few cups of joe while I waited to leave. I thought about that Flintstones episode where Fred propped his eyes open with toothpicks (you know the one, I'm sure). I wondered if that would work in real life.

Here I went again. I hopped in the car and drove the twenty-five minutes back over to Apalachicola . . . only to discover that the *store* opened at 9:00 a.m., but the *pharmacy* didn't open until 11:00 a.m. (Say it with me, "ARRRGG!") I was beyond upset. Sleep deprived, vacation deprived, the sarcasm flew out of my mouth faster than I could catch it. I coolly suggested to the manager that they give the pharmacist a pager when they couldn't reach him at home: "It's a pretty novel idea, I know." What a jerk I can be!

So, I stomped out into the parking lot. "Great. Now I have to wait two hours. What will I do? It's not worth it to drive back to the island. It's Sunday, and nothing is open. I guess I'll . . . I'll . . . I'll just go to church!" So, me and my bad attitude went driving around looking for a place to go. I decided that "Friendship Baptist" didn't fit my emotional state, so I drove past it and on to First Baptist. This beautiful little white church building just radiated warmth. Here I was, in denim shorts, my "Sail fast, live slow" tee shirt, my Nikes, no make-up, and a baseball hat—in my Sunday best—going to church. I thought, *well, it will be amusing at least to see how people react when they see me.* Anything for comic relief at this point.

I walked into the church, down the hall, and ran into a couple of older ladies. They just smiled at me as if I truly *was* dressed in my Sunday best and directed me to a Sunday school class. A nice man in the room was getting ready to teach. He reached his hand out, gave me a big smile, and said, "Hello!" I introduced myself, told him my situation, and he warmly welcomed me. He told me to get some breakfast across the hall before class. Ah, there's nothing like church food brought from home. All greeted me with open arms. They were concerned and wanted to know if they could help me. "Just pray for me," *and my bad attitude*, I thought.

I had a wonderfully full tummy and sat back to surprisingly enjoy the best discussion on *Revelation* I've ever had. After class they invited me to stay for church. I really wanted to, but Casey really needed his medicine. I had to get back. How strange. I came to God's house in a foul mood from a frustrating situation of waiting and was so blessed that I didn't want to leave. I sheepishly went back to the drugstore and apologized to the manager for how I had behaved earlier. I got the medicine and was back to the island and was sitting on the beach by noon. It certainly was an unusual experience. But the central theme to the entire series of events was the waiting: waiting for the happy times, waiting too late for medical care, waiting on sleep to get care, waiting for stores to open and people to arrive. But through it all, did I once wait for God's blessing? Did I once try and see what I could miss while I waited? I was given a gift to be loved and accepted and cared for just as I was by God's people. Few things warm the heart more than that. Look what I would have missed . . . if I had not been required to wait.

> "But let patience have her perfect work, that ye may be perfect and entire, wanting nothing" (James 1:4, KJV).

What is it about waiting that we resist so much? Why does it just seem to suck the joy out of us sometimes? Shouldn't we get a clue that waiting is woven into the fabric of everyday life so we can just get over ourselves? Reflect on your past 24 hours. How many times did you wait: on people, on traffic, on schedules, on food, on just time itself? Sometimes I wonder where we think we are going so fast.

Can waiting hurt you? Well, I guess waiting too long sometimes can. Like waiting too long to go to the doctor, too long to buy or sell in the stock market, too long to flip the chicken on the grill. But I mean just waiting in general—does it *really* hurt you? Like waiting for that acceptance letter, or waiting for the right weather to go out, or waiting to get married, or for that baby to be born, or just waiting to make that life-altering decision until you have all the info you need. If you're like me, you wait . . . and you think about having to wait . . . and you fight the process. It's like we're so expectant to see what's just around the corner with each facet of our lives, whether it's a traffic light or that job offer, that we can't enjoy the process. So, we miss the blessings all around us along the way because of our waiting-induced bad attitudes.

Here's what is so ridiculous about my waiting rant so I could get to the beach. Guess what I did when I finally planted my toes in the sand? I waited. When I'm at the beach, I just sit and look out to sea. It's like I'm expectantly waiting for the next wave or the next pelican dive, or the next dolphin fin to emerge. I sit and I look, and I wait. Even on vacation, being where I most love to be at the beach, I can't stop playing the waiting game. Isn't this a funny paradox about my medicine-waiting story? I didn't like waiting because it kept me from getting to the beach so I could sit and look out to sea . . . and wait.

I wait to get hot enough to go into the water for a dip. In the water I wait for just the right wave to body surf onto shore. Then I wait to dry off to reapply sunscreen. Then I wait for the right time to turn and even out my tan. I wait for lunch or for that breeze to blow a little harder. Then I sit and do some more staring out to sea. Maybe the waiting game is one we all play because there is no end to the game. But at the end of my vacation, I surely do feel good and rested even after all my reflex waiting by the sea all day. Could it be that while I'm soaking up rays, I'm soaking up blessings for my spirit? I think so.

Perhaps there is an explanation in this quote by Mortimer Adler: "You have to allow a certain amount of time in which you are doing nothing in order to have things occur to you, to let your mind think."[1]

Well, what do you know? Waiting gets a face-lifted image: waiting is necessary. Waiting is productive. Waiting is *good* for you. Later, I'll talk about the importance of choosing to be still. One time of being still is a renewing choice; the other time of waiting is not. Why can't the times of unwanted stillness be just as renewing? Maybe we're given times of stillness in our lives when we don't realize that it's what we need most at that point in time.

Have you ever thought about the waiting game that others across time have played, or rather have unwillingly been forced to play? Take Bible characters for instance. David was called to be king, but it took ten years before he actually became king. Abraham was told he would father a nation, but it took decades for that to happen. Joseph had to wait while sitting in a dark prison for years, before someone remembered he was good at interpreting dreams, and before he was made second highest ruler in the land of Egypt.

There was poor Noah. God instructed him to build the ark a hundred years before endless rain was predicted on the weather channel. He had to endure the ridicule of those who thought he was off his rocker. I'm sure at times Noah himself thought he was, too. Most people think that Noah was just stuck on board for forty days and forty nights, but that's only how long it *rained.* He then had to watch and wait until the floodwaters covered the mountains. His family and all of Earth's surviving creation no doubt went stir crazy, but no one could get off the boat until all that water receded from the mountains. They were stuck on board for a *year.* When Noah sent out the dove, it returned with an olive branch to let him know new growth had begun, but he still had to wait another week before it was safe for his floating zoo to stampede off the Ark.

Don't get me started on Moses, the waiting king. He waited in Midian for decades before getting a job offer from God. He didn't want to go. Even when he did go, he had to wait and wait and wait through a ton of plagues for Pharaoh to comply. Then he had to wait in the desert for forty years with a bunch of cranky Israelites until they reached the Promised Land.

Why in the world does God work that way with those He calls to accomplish a task? If it's for God and His work, why not get on with it? Why the delay?

> Never think that God's delays are God's denials. Hold on; hold fast; hold out. Patience is genius. —*Comte de Buffon*[2]

I've concluded that it's many times about the person He calls, not about the calling itself. He'll take anyone with an obedient spirit, no matter how green, messy, or ignorant they may be. But once you sign on, He's got to put you through basic training to get you in shape to operate with His high standards, methods, and ways. Perhaps you don't have the mental knowledge, the spiritual maturity, or the emotional depth needed to accomplish what He has in mind. Maybe you want to call the shots in how things proceed, and God knows you'll fall flat on your face unless *He's* the one in charge. He's got to test your commitment and your endurance to see what kind of stuff you're made of for the long haul. Perhaps it is for *you* to see what you're made of . . . for God already knows. This basic training always, always grows you in maturity, self-confidence, and ultimately, dependence on God.

So, while we're waiting and getting upset at God for not doing anything, could it be that *we* are the holdup? Is it us whom He's waiting on? To show we trust Him so He can trust us with what He's about to do? To prepare us mentally, having thoroughly thought things through? To prepare us emotionally, with a solid resolve and conviction to move ahead? To just grow up a little? Or a lot? Spring showers can pop up in an afternoon. Hurricanes take days. I think God makes us wait because He's got bigger ideas in mind. Plus, His timing is always perfect. He's never too early or too late. He can see what's coming down the pike in eternity, so He knows the right moment in time to get you moving.

Going Nowhere Fast

There is no more miserable place for a sailor to be than in the doldrums. Ever been there? I mean the *real* doldrums. I've been to the metaphorical ones, but thank goodness, never to the place that gave us the less-than-exciting word. Here's the encyclopedia definition: "Equatorial belt of calms, area around the earth centered slightly north of the equator between the two belts of trade winds. The large amount of solar radiation that arrives at the earth in this area causes intense heating of the land and ocean. This heating results in the rising of warm, moist air; low air pressure; cloudiness, high humidity; light, variable winds; and various forms of severe weather, such as thunderstorms and squalls. Hurricanes originate in this region. The doldrums are also noted for calms, periods when the winds disappear, trapping sailing vessels for days or weeks."[3] Ok, yeah—that makes me want to call my travel agent and book a cruise *there*. What a nightmare to be stuck in the doldrums!

Here you are, clipping along at a refreshing speed, sails full and boat cresting the blue waves on the big blue sea. Then . . . utter calm. No wind. Sea of glass. The sails just loosely hang on the mast. The sun turns hot. Your skin gets sticky. Your patience wears thin. You're forced to do something, anything, to feel productive. You clean the fiberglass, you treat the teakwood, you mend the sails, you eat, you sleep, you try to read . . . you go crazy with boredom! I've heard some stories of sailors stuck in the doldrums, and I don't envy their time there.

Robin Lee Graham was sailing solo around the world when he got stuck for nearly forty days in the doldrums aboard his sailboat, *Dove*. It would be hard enough enduring the doldrums when you had company—someone to talk to. But Robin only had his pet cats aboard, who were just as bored as he. When giving advice on how anyone could endure the doldrums, he warned people that they might return as raving lunatics. Robin recorded in his log that he just stared at his charts and couldn't even muster the energy to eat. Although the waters were smooth as glass, Robin's mental state deteriorated into a meltdown when he couldn't lower the mainsail from the jammed rigging. In his frustration, he broke his flashlight and almost slashed up his sails with a diving knife. He later realized that stillness without tension in life can indeed lead to madness. He opined that we must have a goal or something to work toward, otherwise it's like sailing forever through the doldrums. Have you been in doldrums like that? All alone, sometimes going crazy, getting angry and frustrated, even wondering what your goal truly is?

Thies and Kicki Matzen were on their boat, *Wanderer III,* when they got stuck in the doldrums. In their *Cruising World* story article, "In the Kingdom of Silence," Thies remarked, "Many times we've eased into windlessness, nurturing our patience to take a good look at eternity."[4] But this time it would be twenty-three days for these sailors to nurture that patience.

"At times the silent wind steadied between zero and six knots, peaking during the night, when it detected our yearning eyes, it dozed off wearily. It became pure torture to chase half a knot each time that cursed wind deigned to lower its breath . . . We never gained momentum. We waited. We touched boredom. We never reached vitality."

But hope always comes. On their nineteenth day they were able to "jump charts," meaning that the coast of New Guinea got larger on the map as they were able to mark their position on a larger nautical chart. They were drifting, and painfully drifting, but "finally, there was hope." They gradually began to see land; the Cape of Good Hope was coming into view. "All our hopes had been projected onto it for such a long time. Surely no cape carries such a name for no reason."

Just as their boat coasted right off the cape, the wind appeared. "Then suddenly, as if we'd crossed an invisible threshold, air descended from the hills, and it enchantingly started to blow. There was wind, real wind." These sailors smiled, and their hearts sang as they coasted into the harbor of their destination, true basic training survivors of the doldrums.

The winds of grace are always blowing. We only have to raise our sails and catch the breeze. —*Unknown*

If you're stuck in the doldrums, take heart. Remember—hurricanes originate in the doldrums. A place dead to wind is the birthplace for the mightiest winds of them all. When God is serious about doing something mighty in our lives, many times He has to get us started in this kingdom of silence. No, it's not fun. Yes, it can be trying and very uncomfortable. But do the doldrums last forever? The answer is no. And don't forget, there are incredible blessings waiting for you during this time of still winds. The winds of grace are always blowing even when the winds of progress are still.

The winds of grace can bring so many blessings into our sails! Time is a powerful gift. Why then do we try to rush it? Have you ever made a mistake when rushing into something? Ever messed up a batch of chocolate chip cookies (my favorite) by missing an ingredient because you were in a hurry? A treat turned into tastebud torture. What about something a little more challenging? I know—did you ever use those CliffsNotes in school? Those yellow little literary shortcut books that help answer questions to the test without reading the book? Ever miss the test questions anyway? I can answer yes to all the above. Not only did I miss the blessing of expanding my mind by reading some really great books, but I also cheated myself of better grades. I should have just taken the time and read the book.

But these are small matters of not waiting. What about more important matters? What if Michelangelo had just thrown some paint up on the ceiling of the Sistine Chapel and not waited months and months to plan and complete a good work? What if Christopher Columbus had turned back the day before he sighted land? Obviously, waiting for a project to be completed and completed well certainly doesn't mean we sit still. We must be actively doing something, but we must wait for the right time for completion. This can be laborious and agonizing, I know.

I've been in the doldrums for six months, trying to write this chapter on the doldrums! I've been stuck with still winds of inspiration. I've been writing this book for two and a half years. At times throughout this writing cruise I've thought, "OK, I *must* be finished by now." But there was always more that God wanted me to learn, always more He wanted me to share. I've tried to keep busy, always working on some aspect of the book. But there have been times when I've done nothing but wait. The winds of inspiration are blowing once again, and my writing sails are full.

Sometimes there are life events that put us in doldrums where there is nothing to do *but* wait. You've done all you can do, and the situation is no longer in your hands. Families in hospital waiting rooms can tell you that. Parents waiting on prodigal children to return home can tell you that. You have no control over the situation and are bound by the hands of time. What possible blessings can come from doldrums such as these? Oh, they are there. A realization that a loving family or a close group of friends surrounds you. An encounter with the true God who loves you so and who will give you that peace which passes all understanding. A strength in your spirit and a countenance in your character that you didn't have before entering the doldrums. An appreciation for people or things you once took for granted. There are always blessings to be found in the doldrums.

You can't force the winds to blow. But you *can* pray for them to kick up again. And they eventually will, bringing you to your desired destination. So, for now, ". . . let patience have its perfect work, that you may be perfect and complete, lacking nothing" (James 1:4, NKJV). Try to enjoy this waiting time of basic training. Don't struggle with it. Soak up the blessings to be had. Sit on the beach and stare out to sea. As Robert Frost observed, you might not be able to look out far, nor in deep, but when was that ever a bar to any watch you keep?

Wait and sea. You will always make it to the Cape of Good Hope if your hope is in God and His winds of grace. But then be ready . . . for the sail of a lifetime!

PART TWO

SMOOTH SAILING

"Give me this glorious ocean life, this salt-sea life, this briny, foamy life, when the sea neighs and snorts, and you breathe the very breath that the great whales respire! Let me roll around the globe, let me rock upon the sea, let me race and pant out my life, with an eternal breeze astern, and an endless sea before!"

—Herman Melville[1]

Twenty years from now you will be more disappointed by
the things you didn't do than by the ones you did do.
So, throw off the bowlines. Sail away from the safe harbor.
Catch the trade winds in your sails. Explore. Dream. Discover.

—Mark Twain[1]

Chapter 5

RUN THE GUNNELS

One of my favorite movies is *Dead Poets Society*. Robin Williams plays an English teacher who ignites a passion for poetry in his class of eager young students. While introducing himself to the students he recites a line from a Walt Whitman poem, "Oh Captain, My Captain," giving his students the option of addressing him with this endearing moniker or by name. In this powerful scene he takes his students to a hall of class pictures of generations long gone. The pictures depict young men with eyes full of promise and ambition. Williams asks his students, "Do you hear it? Listen hard. They are speaking." Then he begins to hoarsely whisper, *"Car-pe. Car-pe. Diem. Carpe . . . diem."* He explains that this phrase is Latin for "Seize the day."

The young students take this term *"carpe diem"* to heart. As the movie continues, each student conquers the fear or obstacle that has kept him from realizing his individual dream. They take risks. They "just do it." They go for the gusto. Or, in sailor terminology, their captain teaches them to "run the gunnels."

What does "run the gunnels" mean? Before I explain, let me give you a sailboat anatomy lesson. Along the lines of the deck of a sailboat are rims called gunnels. When a sailboat is really moving fast across the water with strong winds, it can lean, or "heel," way over. The gunnels of the boat will lean toward or skim the surface of the water. This position is called running the gunnels. *This* is real sailing! This is when it gets fun. When you are running the gunnels, you are holding on for a wild ride over the waves. You must secure everything, both on deck and in the cabin, or things will topple over. Yee-ha, ride 'em, cowboy! This is when a sailboat can take you on the sail of your life.

This is exactly what a sailboat is designed to do. A sailboat has a keel below the waterline that is filled with several thousand pounds of lead for ballast. This ballast is what enables a boat to run the gunnels without danger of tipping over. So, although the people aboard may have a nervous jolt of adrenaline or a feeling of their stomach dropping, the boat itself is happy as a clam. The *boat* knows it can handle the running of the gunnels because that is what it was designed to do. It knows that it would take a 50-foot wave or 100 mile-per-hour-plus winds to tip it over. But even if such extreme conditions occur, this boat also knows that it has an ace up its sleeve. That ace is called "the righting moment."

If a sailboat tips too far over, the keel takes charge and forces the boat to right itself. Even if the boat turns completely upside down in the water, the ballast in the keel will take over the situation to bring the boat right side up. If you have seen the movie *The Perfect Storm*, there is a righting moment depicted during the storm. A West Sail 32 sailboat turns completely upside down with mast underwater but rolls back upright to the surface. Although not shown in the movie of this true story, after the passengers aboard were airlifted off the sailboat during the storm, the boat was later found on the beach with the hull perfectly intact.

If a sailboat is designed and built correctly, it will have three inherent abilities. I've told you about running the gunnels and the righting moment, which are two of those abilities. But without the third ability, neither of those two would be possible.

The third inherent ability is maintaining even keel. When sitting in still waters with sails down, the boat will have even displacement in the water. It will not lean over lopsided but will sit on top of the water in a stable, secure position. When a boat is either moored at anchor or at dock, maintaining even keel is vital. Not only does it give sailors rest and safe harboring, even keel shows that the boat is seaworthy. Maintaining even keel comes entirely from the ballast held within the keel itself.

> A ship in the harbor is safe . . . but that's not what ships were made for. —*Unknown*

Guess what? God made you with the same three abilities as a sailboat. He designed you to have an even keel, to run the gunnels, and to have a righting moment. But here is the requirement. Just as with a sailboat, God must be the stabilizing ballast in your keel for the other two abilities to work as they should. With God as your ballast, your vessel is stable and steady and secure. But God made you to do so much more.

God instilled in you the ability and the desire to run the gunnels. That's where dreams, goals, and hopes reside—in your gunnels. It's when you get those gunnels in the water that you can make those dreams come alive. You can't do so if you remain at even keel in safe harbor. It requires risk and stepping out. Many times, it requires waiting for fair winds to blow. It requires securing everything on deck or in the cabin, so things don't topple over. It requires being willing to experience that nervous jolt of adrenaline or that roller coaster drop in your stomach.

> The sea is dangerous and its storms terrible, but these obstacles have never been sufficient reason to remain ashore . . . unlike the mediocre, intrepid spirits seek victory over those things that seem impossible . . . it is with an iron will that they embark on the most daring of all endeavors to meet the shadowy future without fear and conquer the unknown. —*Ferdinand Magellan*[2]

Stop and think a minute about the progress man has made over the centuries. We've gone from transportation by horse across the country to transportation by rocket to the moon. We've gone from communicating via agonizingly slow mail letters across the state to communication by instant email across the world. We've gone from painful surgery without anesthetic to painless surgery while asleep. We've gone from thinking the world was flat to *knowing* it is round. Do you think that the minds that gave birth to such progress did so by remaining at even keel? Of course not! They did so by running the gunnels.

Do you have a dream or a desire to do something great in your life? It might be with a career, or it might simply be just for fun. If you are pursuing that dream, good for you! It's quite a rush, isn't it? If you are not in pursuit of your dream, why is that? What is stopping you? Time? Money? Motivation? A lack of encouragement? The seeming impossibility of the dream becoming a reality? A fear of failure or disappointment? Could it be . . . risk aversion?

> One doesn't discover new lands without consenting to lose sight of the shore for a very long time. —*Andre Gide*[3]

> To hope is to risk pain. To try is to risk failure. But risk must be taken because the greatest hazard in life is to risk nothing. The person who risks nothing does nothing, has nothing, and is nothing. He may avoid suffering and sorrow, but he simply cannot learn, feel, change, grow, live, or love. Chained by his addictions, he's a slave. He has forfeited his greatest trait, and that is his individual freedom. Only the person who risks is free. —*Leo Buscaglia*[4]

I couldn't have said it better myself. Andre and Leo are both right. We were made with the ability to risk. And guess what? There is always a positive result whenever you take a risk. It may not be the end result that you had in mind. It may be a newly found sense of confidence within your spirit for having just given it your best try. Many times, it is the *process* of risk that brings the greatest reward.

Still don't like that word, "risk?" Ok, how about a synonym? Try "faith" on for size. Does that feel more comfortable? We don't usually equate faith with the dangers of risk. You know why? Faith equals risk plus a safety net. Faith is running the gunnels, knowing full well that the righting moment will be there if we need it. Faith is complete confidence in the design of your vessel, and in the ballast in your keel.

You may have never considered "faith" to be exciting, but I'm here to tell you, there is no greater rush than to go after your dreams with God at your side. If your faith is entrusted entirely to the will of God's purpose and direction for your life, there's no way you can lose! He knows what He is doing, and He knows what is best for you in each and every life experience. He's your heavenly Father! He wants the best for His child and will make sure you have the best if you leave the choices up to Him. What I have found in my life experience is that sometimes the dreams I have held up as supreme goals were sometimes realized. But other times, those dreams were replaced by even better realities because God had better ideas in mind. I've learned to trust His closed doors far more than the open ones.

So, let's get back to your dreams and ambitions for a moment. Talk with God about it, and then figure out what it is that is keeping you in safe harbor. Identify those restricting bowlines, and figure out a departure plan A, B, C . . . or Z if you must. As Twain said, release those bowlines, go, do, and explore. Run the gunnels! But don't wait; do it NOW. There's a good reason to get on with it.

I like the way American business philosopher, Jim Rohn, describes the urgency of taking action: "Engaging in genuine discipline requires that you develop the ability to take action. You don't need to be hasty if it isn't required, but you don't want to lose much time either. Here's the time to act: when the idea is hot and the emotion is strong. Take action as soon as possible, before the feeling passes and before the idea dims. If you don't, here's what happens. You fall prey to the law of diminishing intent. We intend to take action when the idea strikes us. We intend to do something when the emotion is high. But if we don't translate that intention into action fairly soon, the urgency starts to diminish. A month from now the passion is cold. A year from now it can't be found."[5]

Excellent wisdom from Mr. Rohn. I have experienced exactly what he describes here, as I'm sure you have. I have even experienced this on a spiritual level. Sometimes God impresses me to do things that ignite a passion in me, such as reaching out to someone in need, but I sit on it. And the opportunity goes away. I lose the intended blessing, both for that someone, and for myself. I always regret it. So, I have really tried to work better at staying in tune with God's gentle prodding. I try to get up and do it right then, whatever it is, no matter how crazy it seems. I have never regretted taking action when impressed to do so. The blessing I receive always blows me away.

> What lies behind us and what lies before us are tiny matters compared to what lies within us. —*Unknown*

I don't think God instills dreams in our hearts without giving us the ability to make them become reality. If He didn't give us the ability, it wouldn't be congruent with the design package He gave our vessels. Yes, we might have to wait for fair winds to propel us forward. But that doesn't mean we have to just sit in the harbor. Go out there and be ready for when the winds kick up. And remember that sometimes it is in the waiting that we become the most prepared. We have time to think about how to proceed correctly and to crystallize our dreams.

Don't be afraid to take risks or step out in faith. If you maintain God as your stabilizing ballast, you will always have a righting moment if you go too far. God made this world and this life so big and detailed that it could not be totally seen or experienced in the course of a lifetime. What a blessing that is! Just think of the possibilities. If you're a nature lover, there's an enormous world to go see and discover. If your world of interest lies in one of the arts, go pursue and explore it. Teach yourself; learn, grow, master a talent. If intellectual prowess is your world to conquer, read, educate your mind; seek wisdom from the experts. If athleticism or a new sport is your dream, get the equipment, watch how it's done and do it. If you want to become a master gardener, paint your thumb green! If you have a passion for helping people, find a way to help and then do it.

I may run the gunnels too much. Sometimes I think I should experience a little more even keel while at rest in safe harbor. But at this point in my life, I want to do and see and experience all I can. I'll let you in on a secret I've discovered. When you begin to let yourself experience the exhilaration of running the gunnels as you were made to do, you'll get greedy to experience it even more. That "good greed" will spill over into all aspects of your life.

I have become increasingly athletic over the years, gaining interest in trying new outdoor sports. I wasn't always this way, but once I tasted the fun of a new experience, my desire to do more of it increased. I even want to try things that I know will be hard, and for which I might not have the skill, but the fun comes in the trying. Windsurfing and rock climbing are on my life to-do list. I may discover that I don't like or can't do either one, but how will I ever know if I don't try?

Let me encourage you to create a life to-do list. Start a list of things you want to do as life goes on. As you discover something new, add it to the list. As you do it, check it off, and proceed to the next item. There's something about putting dreams, goals, and plans down in writing, which gives you a first step in making those things happen. And it feels great to check them off! Your list might not be filled with physical challenges or adventures. It may be filled with books to read, places to go, talents to try, people to help, etc. But it will be filled with the dreams that God has instilled in your spirit as a unique individual.

So, begin. But don't get all wild and unwise in your actions. Run the gunnels but in the right things and in the right time. Use sound judgment, not throwing all caution to the wind. Before sailors get out in open water to run the gunnels, the sails are set, items are secured above and below deck, the dock lines are stowed away, the weather is monitored, and the course is known in advance. Being prepared is what makes it fun.

The choice of staying in safe harbor or running the gunnels is always yours. You can stay where you are, but again, Twain was right. You will look back twenty years from now with regret. To know what you could have been, done, or accomplished and didn't—what a travesty.

Listen to your heart. Do you hear it? *"Car-pe . . . diem. Carpe diem.* Oh Captain, my Captain, help me to run the gunnels!"

May you have the hindsight to know where you've been,
the foresight to know where you're going, and the insight
to know when you're going too far.

—Irish Proverb

Chapter 6

STAY THE COURSE

Course Heading: Dublin, Ireland, 6/11/00

I love to fly, but it makes me do really weird things. There's something about being confined to an airplane seat for an extended period that turns me into a sort of prisoner. I enjoy it more in the cockpit where I can see what's going on. I don't like being restricted, so back in my passenger seat I'm eager for anything that comes my way, whether I really want it or not. Maybe it's the price of the airline ticket. I might as well take full advantage of every penny.

For instance, the nuts. I don't sit around at home and eat peanuts if they are placed in front of me. But put me on a plane, and I'll eat every one of those mixed nuts in a cup, even the kind I don't like, as if they were the last food I'll ever eat. I'll accept whatever is offered, no matter what time it's offered.

I am writing this on a flight from Atlanta to Dublin, Ireland. We are on our way over to spend two weeks with the Cote clan, to enjoy the Emerald Isle. Our flight was delayed so we ate dinner in the airport. Then we ate dinner again, an in-flight dinner at 10:00 p.m. I'm sitting here stuffed, watching my son Alex sleeping next to me. He was the wise one. He fell asleep before our second dinner got here.

I, on the other hand, sat eagerly in my prisoner's chair, waiting to be served a roll at 10:15, salad at 10:30, and pasta at 11:00. Like I was even hungry to begin with. I had to force the delicious stuff down. At least I said no when the ice cream sundae cart rolled by at midnight. I feel as though I should get a medal for that self-denial of pleasure in my prison chair. So, here I sit at 12:30 a.m., sipping decaf coffee and eating the chocolate truffle that I accepted because I didn't want to hurt the flight attendant's feelings with a second rejection. I'm eating out of my ordinary diet and staying awake out of my ordinary schedule simply because my surroundings have changed. I'm also on vacation, so that entitles me to alter the way I do things anyway.

I love watching the "air show" screen that shows the aerial map of where our plane is located above the Earth. You can watch the little white plane slowly creep across the screen, knowing exactly how far you've come, and what your current position is. The screen also tells you the time, how many minutes you've been in the air, your ground speed, tail wind, and estimated arrival time. How cool is that?! I bet Christopher Columbus would have *loved* to have had one of these toys. Of particular interest to me is the dotted line in front of our pictorial plane showing the charted course to Dublin. It's quite a comfort for me to see that the course has been well planned, is being followed to a T, and will guide us safely into Dublin by morning (8:45 a.m. to be exact). I see other points of interest on this aerial map. Iceland is looming large to the north of us. And two other locales, Barcelona and Casablanca, are highlighted to the south of us.

We are in the middle of the north Atlantic Ocean . . . in the middle of the darkest night . . . but I'm not worried. The pilots know how to fly this plane, and they are staying the course. Staying the course means not altering your destination and not compromising how you operate while you are en route. I know that we won't end up in Iceland, which is a relief because I didn't bring my snow boots. And I know we won't end up in Barcelona or Casablanca, which would be lovely to see, but those aren't destinations for this trip. I know we will end up in Dublin as we have planned. I've crossed the ocean at night many times, but there was one trip in particular that was uniquely memorable.

Course Heading:
Flashback to Bimini, Bahamas, 6/20/80

In 1980, I crossed the ocean at night in a sailboat. We had chartered a 35-foot Pearson sailboat out of Fort Lauderdale to go to the Bimini Islands, Bahamas. The adrenaline was surging through our veins as we left the marina at 9:30 p.m. to head out on the 51-mile trip over deep, dark waters on our own. I remember leaving the harbor and watching the swirling wake behind us lit by harbor lights that slowly dimmed as we got farther from shore.

We were in deep ocean swells in no time. I wanted a prime seat for this experience, so I stayed in the cockpit where I made my bed for the night. But I didn't sleep much for *this* ocean crossing, either. The waves were so close to the stern, I let my hand slice through the fizzing water next to my bed, and I noticed something unusual. The water was glowing from phosphorus plankton. I never knew such low-end-of-the-food chain creatures could be so beautiful. Individually by themselves, they can't be seen, but put them all together, and they celebrate to light up the ocean!

We didn't have a nice TV to show us our position and course laid out on a dotted line. We had to navigate across the ocean by dead reckoning. Dead reckoning involves using time, speed, and distance to chart your position. We also had to compensate for the Gulf Stream that crossed our path. Like trying to sail across a flowing river, you can't go straight across. You must aim lower so the stream will bring you back higher.

This nighttime navigation had to be right, and it had to be monitored frequently. We had to stay the course, or we could end up far out into the ocean away from land. When morning came, we got a little taste of what Christopher Columbus must have felt. As the sun peered over the horizon, we still had no sight of land. Apprehension was understandable. What if we had overcompensated for the Gulf Stream? What if we had miscalculated any of the variables of time, speed, and distance? What if we had veered off course? What if? What if? What if?

At first, we strained our eyes so hard to see land that I think we saw mirages. Was that land? No, just waves. A little time passed. Is that land? Hmmm . . . a little . . . bit . . . farther . . . and . . . we'll be able . . . to see . . . LAND! BIMINI STRAIGHT AHEAD! We all glowed as much as the plankton. We did it! And a beautiful week of island hopping awaited us as our reward.

The Bimini Islands were indeed beautiful. My brother Joe picked up a big red starfish right under the boat where we were anchored. He wanted to keep it but put it back after I pitched a fit. We went snorkeling on an old shipwreck, ate conch fritters at the Red Lion Pub, and enjoyed sailing amidst the sheer beauty of this island paradise.

We sailed over to Cat Cay, and as we anchored, I jumped over to snorkel to shore. I followed the stingrays that were coasting over the grassy area that dead-ended into white sand in shallow water at the beach. I didn't pay a lot of attention to where I was. I was watching the rays and the pretty fish swimming around. I suddenly felt uneasy and looked up to see three large barracuda floating straight ahead of me. They were blocking my path to the beach. I wanted to turn and swim at top speed back to the boat, but that would have been risky. I had to stay put . . . and just wait.

Barracuda are curious fish, and if you can bore them, they'll go away eventually. They are totally creepy as they stay in one position, with mouths opening and closing to breathe, flashing their razor-sharp teeth. I hate these guys! At least I had taken off all my jewelry, which usually catches their beady little blank eyes. So, I floated on the surface, and the three bad-guy barracudas and I had a stare down. I guess I won because they eventually swam off. I made it to the beach, but I never could journey back to the boat without fear of seeing them again. And see them again, I did.

I learned not to go it alone—always have a partner when snorkeling. I had been too impatient to wait for anybody else and had endangered myself. I also learned to be extremely aware of my surroundings, especially in new territory where I am totally ignorant of what could be lurking about. I learned to stand my ground and be patient. Talk about a crash course in staying the course! My reward was making it to the beach uninjured. After that scare I was able to enjoy the rest of the week. I was a bit wiser and mindful of the dangers that can lurk amid beauty.

The time in these islands was wonderful. But nothing, nothing could match the spectacular sunset that we experienced as we set sail back across the ocean a week later. I have never seen more hues of red, pink, orange, yellow, blue, and white mixed together on such an enormous canvas of a horizon. Sailing back to Fort Lauderdale from Bimini at night, we navigated and stayed the course just as before. And we arrived safely just as before.

Course Heading: Flashback to Bonaire, Netherlands Antilles, 7/2/80

This was truly the summer of incredible trips. A week after we returned from our cruise to Bimini, we were blessed to join our dear friends, the

Turneys, for a trip to Bonaire, in the Netherlands Antilles. One of the coolest things about the trip was that we flew there in a six-passenger Cessna 421. I had never been in a small plane before, so it was exciting. I especially liked the turbulence. As everyone else was turning white, I was yelling for more. Turbulence, yeah, baby! Later in the trip, I got to sit in the co-pilot's seat when we buzzed over to Caracas, Venezuela, from Bonaire. Wow, what a rush! Now *that* is the plane seat I like.

What was even more exciting than the turbulence was our flight path. Before flying down the chain of Caribbean islands to Haiti for refueling and then on to Bonaire, we flew right over the course we had sailed the week before, from Fort Lauderdale to Bimini. We were able to see the 51-mile path we had sailed at night, as well as the various islands we had been to. The water was so blue, clear, and beautiful, and the white sands looked so inviting even from high altitudes. But you couldn't see any bad-guy barracudas, which was a good thing.

What an interesting sight; the same route looked so short from the air and *was* short from the air. We crossed in minutes by plane what had taken hours by boat. And it was so easy to see the appropriate course that led us from Fort Lauderdale to Bimini. Makes you wonder—maybe if we tried to see things from a higher vantage point in life, like from God's viewpoint, we'd see how simple and clear staying the course really is. There's something about seeing the big picture that puts life's geography into perspective. The small details that we worry so much about seem to just disappear and lose their importance. There's a great lesson here.

Staying the course is vital in the important issues of life. You have to know your starting point A, your destination point B, and how you are going to get from one to the other. If you veer off course, the consequences can be serious. Whether it be the course of school, of work, of marriage, of raising a child, of commitments, of moral choices, or of decisions of great importance, you won't succeed in getting to point B unless you stay the course. The kicker is that these are the courses that are the hardest to make. But nothing worthwhile comes easy, does it? Perhaps it's the difficulty that makes the object of our desire so worthwhile in the first place. The difficulty certainly tests us to see how badly we *really* want something.

There are always deceivingly easier side routes along the way to tempt us, especially when we are so tired or discouraged. Escapism can always be found in every circumstance, and it is always an option. But it's an option only if copping out is your style. Escapism seems to hit most strongly at our greatest points of vulnerability. And escapism is just as ugly—and dangerous—as bad-guy barracudas.

I want to qualify this philosophy before we proceed. There are times when it becomes evident that the right thing to do is to alter the course and take a different tack or angle to reach your destination. When sailing from one destination to another, sometimes the prevailing winds are not blowing from the right direction to fill your sails to move you forward. You can't change the direction of the wind, but you can change the direction of the boat to capture the wind. Instead of sailing a straight path, you must zigzag back and forth, or "tack." You will still get to your destination; it will just take longer. The point is that you don't alter your destination; you just alter the way you get there.

Let me put it in landlubber terms. If you have a vital appointment to keep, and your driving route to get there has been blocked by a wreck, what do you do? You find an alternate route to take you around the wreck so you can still get to your vital appointment.

When you are trying to stay the course in the big issues of life, don't alter your destination, but be prepared to change your tack if necessary. Also, don't even go there alone (remember the snorkeling lesson). Be aware of your surroundings, monitor your course heading frequently, and always be well provisioned for the trip. There are many provisions out there to help you, such as books on marriage, career, and self-help in general. I would encourage you to read all you can, especially the Supreme Life Guidebook, the Bible. Knowledge and wisdom are powerful allies. But for now, I'm going to give you three key provisions for the trip, along with three scenarios for staying the course in school, a career, and marriage.

Course Provision #1: "I can do everything through him who gives me strength" (Philippians 4:13, NIV).

I remember when I was two weeks away from finishing graduate school; I almost copped out due to sheer exhaustion. I was working fifty hours a week and was in school four nights a week. There was zero time to do anything other than shower, dress, inhale meals, go to work, go to school, and then do all the coursework. Forget the fact that I had a house to run and a husband, a cat, and two Labradors to take care of. I didn't remember what sleep was in those last weeks of school. I got to a point where I just couldn't take it anymore, even though I was so close to graduation. I just didn't care. I wanted to quit and walk away. I just wanted to sit and not think, and the idea of sleep was nice, too.

So, I stepped back and put everything aside one afternoon. I rested and then sat and thought. I thought of the four years of night school I had invested. I thought of the money I had invested (and owed). I thought of how close I was to the finish line. I thought of how great it would be to have that extra-large diploma hanging on my wall and that MS Degree adorning my resume. And then I thought, "What?! Am I *crazy*?! Of course, I'm going to finish what I started. What a fool I would be to stop short of the end and miss the prize that awaits me." (I've used that same self-chat on myself on other life issues over the years, and it works.)

So, yes, I hunkered down and did the work, stayed the course, and finished the course. I received the diploma, the degree, and later, a great job. But most importantly, I received the reward for my inner self of having started at point A, set the path for point B, and stayed the course until I got there. Staying the course in school is *key*. You might have to change the tack of your major or your timeline along the way, but finish what you started. Don't allow yourself to flounder aimlessly in a sea of indecision either.

Course Provision #2: "But one thing I do: Forgetting what is behind and straining toward what is ahead, I press on toward the goal to win the prize for which God has called me heavenward in Christ Jesus" (Philippians 3:13–14, NIV).

Sometimes the course for a successful career requires a lot of tacking. I think this is because sometimes you don't really know what you want to be when you grow up. This isn't the case for everyone. My brother, Joe, knew he wanted to be a doctor from the time he was eight years old and got a biology set for Christmas. So, he knew his destination, but he had a hard course to stick to in order to realize his dream. He now is a fine general surgeon, and I am so proud of him.

I, on the other hand, have so many life interests that I had a hard time deciding what I wanted to do in life. I wanted to be everything from a graphic designer, a singer, a marine biologist to work with dolphins, to a successful businesswoman.

As I started on the career course, I had to take different tacks when it became evident that I either lacked the skill or that certain options weren't reasonable for me. Although I have a creative mind and can envision neat graphics and layout, my hand is not gifted to draw what I see. So graphic design was out. I had a college scholarship in voice and adore singing and music, but I realized that becoming a professional singer or a music teacher were basically my two options, neither of which appealed to me. Science isn't my forte; it grossed me out to dissect frogs, and I was bored to death with chemistry, so marine biology was out. But I finally realized that business, specifically marketing, was where I wanted to be. And the beauty of that tack was that it enabled me to use my God-given skills for my career and other interests peripherally in the process, whether for business or pleasure.

But my career is constantly evolving as I live and grow and learn. Underlying my varied interests has always been a love and a skill to write, so *now* I've entered the world of writing, which is a whole new tack in my life. Do you see the point I'm trying to make? Never stop pursuing an excellent career but change the tack when the winds aren't favorable or when better breezes become available. Forget what is behind and strain ahead to what you should do next, staying the course for nothing but excellence in your life's work.

Course Provision #3: "Let us not become weary in doing good, for at the proper time we will reap a harvest if we do not give up" (Galatians 6:9, NIV).

Marriage is hard. Even a good marriage is hard. When you have two imperfect humans trying to stay on one course, it can be challenging. The counterwinds blow hard, wanting a marriage vessel to never make it to shore. Obstacles like icebergs are ever present and threaten the safety of the vessel. But oh, how sweet it is when you stay on course in a marriage! Staying the course in marriage can and must be a priority. It is one of the most important courses you will ever take. If your marriage is one of happiness and great satisfaction, I applaud you! I celebrate that you have found the secret that so few in our day and age find, the joy of lifelong intimacy in mind, body, and soul with one person. Never underestimate the power of a successful marriage. Not only does it bring you Heaven on Earth, but it is the glue for your family and for society. Without that glue families and society just fall apart. Keep staying the course.

If your marriage is like the Titanic nearing an iceberg, and you feel as if you've made a mistake in the choice of a life partner, it's time to get all hands on deck, sound the alarm bells, and get that ship clear of the iceberg. Titanics don't turn on a dime—this may take some time. It may take weeks, months, or years to turn this ship around, or at least veer off the collision course with the iceberg. Don't expect to do it alone. And don't expect to do it without prayer. A boatload of prayer.

When staying the course in this situation, what you change is not the person (destination) to whom you are married, but how that relationship is administered (the tack). When you get married, you make a vow before God and man that you will remain faithful until death. No cop-outs or escapism permitted here, *especially* when children have been brought into the picture. You may argue, "But God wants me to be happy." EXACTLY. Keep your vow. You made a commitment, which means staying the course and sticking with it, no matter what. You must deal with the obstacles that are making it difficult to stay the course. Grab hold of a major blowtorch to melt that iceberg before you crash into it. No, you can't "change" your spouse. What you can do is make some major tacks. These will be different for varying situations, so I'm only going to give you a couple of starting tacks.

First, remember your commitment, and focus on how you fell in love in the first place. You decided that this person was the one you wanted to be *yours* for life. Recapture those feelings; they are down in the recesses of your heart and mind. Dust them off and put them back on display. I once read that a successful marriage requires falling in love over and over again. It's so true. Try to fall in love with your spouse again. Yes, they may have changed in more ways than one, but that young lover is still there. Second, change *your* behavior. It takes two to tango! I'm sure you're not always a picnic to live with. I know I'm not. Be the best you can be physically, in how you look and how you relate intimately. There is no excuse for not taking pride in how you look and acting upon it. You once were the object of desire for your spouse. You can be again, and age has absolutely nothing to do with it.

Be the best friend you can be. Think about what you would want in a best friend and become it. Listen, and more often than not, hold your tongue. You can always add words, but you can never take them back. Offer help and give support by focusing on your spouse's needs and seeking his or her best interests. Go overboard in expressing love. You'll be amazed at how that blowtorch fires up when love is expressed. Be fun and playful: lighten up and laugh often! And perhaps the key to it all: forgive. I know how hard this is when you are hurting deep inside, especially when your spouse has not met your needs, sought your best interests, or worse yet deflated your self-esteem with biting words. And it is harder still when pride gets in the way as you try to defend yourself. But pride does indeed come before a fall—or an iceberg collision. It can shut off that blowtorch valve of love quickly. Someone once said that when you start *acting* in a loving way, you will start *feeling* in a loving way. Lifetime love isn't an emotional feeling; it's what you *do*, regardless of how you feel at the time.

There's something so liberating about letting go of the right to get even. Jesus frequently talked about loving your enemy and turning the other cheek. Do you know why? It's not so much for the other person's benefit—it's primarily for *yours*. You are the one who gains the power to stop the hurt. The poor behavior of another no longer can hold you captive and consume you emotionally. And something else wonderful happens. Doors of communication start to open. You can see beyond the poor behavior and understand what is driving it, whether it be hurt, disappointment, disillusionment, possibly caused by you in the first place. When this happens, you can move toward fixing the source of the problem. And even if your spouse chooses not to change his or her behavior right away, give it plenty of time. Love is a powerful blowtorch. Icebergs don't stand a chance against it.

What will happen immediately is that you will gain peace in your spirit. Your sense of self-worth will blossom from the fact that you made a commitment and are sticking with it, no matter what. And God will, without a doubt, honor you, take care of you, and bless you beyond belief for staying the course in marriage.

In case you are wondering, yes, I am a realist. I know that as best you try to stay the course, there might be extenuating circumstances that bump you off course. But please listen to me: these need to be the exceptions, not the rule. Our world has adopted a mindset of bowing to the rule and making it conform to any self-gratifying condition we deem most comfortable. That's why our world is so unhappy and is falling apart. Compromising high standards of integrity, honesty, and keeping your word never brings true happiness. But staying the course always will.

There sometimes is physical, mental, or emotional abuse in marriage that should not be endured by the victim. Sometimes a spouse walks out, and there is nothing you can do about it. Sometimes there is unfaithfulness, and you may need to walk away. Sometimes there is substance abuse that threatens the home, and the best solution is to get away from it if the spouse refuses help and endangers the family. There are major life events such as major financial setbacks that can keep you from reaching your destination. Sometimes God even intervenes to let you know you started out on the wrong course heading to begin with in school or in a career. Moses thought his lifelong career was to be a shepherd. Well, it was . . . but not for sheep. God had bigger plans for Moses—to shepherd the nation of Israel. Peter thought his lifelong vocation would be fishing. Well, it was . . . but not for fish. God had bigger plans for Peter—fishing for an entire world of people crying to hear about the One who would save them.

But you know whether it's a true exception, or just a bad-guy barracuda that you can beat. If valid circumstances do throw you off course, take heart. God's grace and love is sufficient, and He will guide your vessel back to where it should be by showing you exactly what, when, and how to do what you need to do to get back on track. Chart a new course as soon as you can. Don't allow anything to discourage you or deter you from living the best life possible. Forget what is behind. Press on toward the goal.

Don't grow weary in doing good. You can do everything through Christ who will give you strength.

The most important course to stay in life is that of following God and maintaining a pure, growing faith. If this primary course is maintained, no matter what, all the others will be easier to stay, no matter what. And if you listen closely, in your heart you will be able to hear God and Heaven applaud you and say, "Well done, good and faithful servant."

OK, take a big, deep breath and let it out slowly. Relax. God designed life to be enjoyed, and enjoyment comes when we've done our jobs well. There's the fun stuff in life to remember that makes the pressure of staying the course in the big stuff easier to manage. If you stay the course in the important matters of life, it's OK, and even *important,* to veer off course in the little stuff. Rewarding yourself with little things on divergent paths along the way is healthy for your psyche. If you colored inside the lines all the time, you'd miss a lot of fun in making the picture even bigger and much more colorful!

So go on vacation and stay up late if you want. Eat a late second dinner if you want, even if you aren't hungry. And if you really want to, go for the midnight ice cream sundae cart, and put a cherry on top!

Course Arrival: Dublin, Ireland, 6/11/00

It's now 8:45 a.m. Nice landing—right on schedule.

As morning breaks autumnal gray another night has passed away,
And in that darkness o'er the deep a single light was in my keep.
A candle in a tempest wind, a lantern's light for me to tend,
A lamp against a restless sea, a beacon's flame eternally.
But now as morning breaks anew my vigil for a time is through,
Another lighthouse keeper though has set a guiding light aglow,
Against the time when we are lost and on an angry sea are tossed,
That all upon this ship might know the way to Him who loves us so.

—Keeper's Prayer, Rod Nichols[1]

Chapter 7

LIGHTHOUSE ILLUMINATION

Class Is in Session

Time for a little mental exercise. Let's do a word association game. Ready? When I say "lighthouse," quick! What's the first word that pops into your mind?

The second word? The third?

Okay, now I want you to picture a lighthouse in your mind. Let's envision one with a round tower, white with spiral black stripes. The top lantern cap is vibrant red. Let's put it on a cliff with crashing waves beneath it. Got it? Now what comes to mind? I imagine that what you think when you hear the word "lighthouse" and what you think when you see one is the same. Some words just embody multiple meanings with powerful singularity.

These are the words that come to mind when I think of lighthouses: comfort, warmth, strength, guidance, consistency, hope, beauty, and protection. When I see or hear the word "lighthouse" I am immediately drawn to the subject. I instantly get the warm fuzzies inside. I think a lot of people do.

What's the deal with lighthouses? I can think of no other man-made general structure that emits that kind of response. Let's see . . . "warehouse," "office building"—nope, nothing. "Monument" gets warmer. Hmmm . . . "house" gets warmer still, but I have to think of a specific house that is dear to me. My neighbor's house is nice, but I don't get the warm fuzzies when I see it.

How about "church?" That's the closest yet, as it shares the attributes of a lighthouse. But it's still not the same. I think the reason that churches aren't all the same is that they house imperfect people trying to worship God with the theology that best suits their understanding of Him. So, adding to the wonderful attributes a church shares with a lighthouse are a level of complexity, and vast differences in belief and direction. I think that must make God sad sometimes. Although He made us unique, and He celebrates our diversity, I'm sure He longs for the day when we will have one voice to praise Him, worship Him, and serve Him.

Ah-ha, Watson! I think I've got it. *Lighthouse*. This has to be it. Forgive me for stating the obvious, but it's the light. And it serves one purpose: to guide lost vessels to safe harbor. It is free to all who seek it out. It requires only to be followed. It is consistent. It is strong. It is beautiful not only on the outside, but for what it does for the one who follows the beacon.

A lighthouse tells you where you are when you are lost. It guides you to shore when it is dark and stormy. Even if you can't see the light in the foggiest of weather, it finds a way to reach you still with its loud, bellowing foghorn or its consistent radio signal. And on clear, bright days a lighthouse stands strongly visible to affirm your position. Seeing a lighthouse in fair weather is important. You know that lighthouse will be there regardless of the weather. A lighthouse is a kind of hero in a way.

But how much do you know about these lighthouse heroes? I didn't realize how little I knew until I did some research. We've had a word pop quiz, how about a little history lesson?

A World Wonder

Lighthouses have guided sailors around shoals for centuries. When do you think the first lighthouse in the world was built? 1700s? 1500s? Unbelievably, it was in 290 B.C. and was one of the Seven Wonders of the Ancient World. The Lighthouse of Alexandria was on the ancient island of Pharos in Egypt and at that time was the tallest building on Earth. It had a mirror that reflected thirty-five miles offshore, which is amazing. The lighthouse remained for centuries, guiding ships into the great harbor with fire at night and the sun's rays during the day. The lighthouse was depicted on Roman coins, and even served as an architectural model for lighthouse construction throughout the region. The ancient lighthouse even gave us an ancient word for the dictionary, "Pharos," which means lighthouse.[2]

Modern Light

In the United States, there are almost six hundred surviving lighthouses that were built on land or in the water. Onshore lighthouses are found on cliffs, peninsulas, islands, or jetties. Offshore lighthouses are anchored to the ocean floor out in deep water.[3] These modern lighthouses were built beginning in the 1700s and were originally manned by resident lighthouse keepers. The story of the keepers is fascinating.

The Keeper

In the early 1800's, the President approved keeper appointments and dismissals. Initially, there were no formal instructions given to keepers, although efficiency was expected. An engineer to the U.S. Light-house Survey, I.W.P. Lewis noted that "the best keepers are found to be old sailors, who are accustomed to watch at night, who are more likely to turn out in a driving snow storm and find their way to the light-house to trim their lamps, because in such weather they know by experience the value of a light, while on similar occasions the landsman keeper would be apt to consider such weather as the best excuse for remaining snug in bed."[4]

Eventually, formal instructions for keepers were developed to include strict regulations regarding operation, behavior, and a dress code of blue-coated uniforms and caps. Keepers were not allowed to leave their post without a supervisor's permission, and even then, for only twenty-four hours.[5] Talk about never being able to leave your work at the office!

Can you imagine what the life of a keeper must have been like? Can you envision putting your children to bed in a tower bedroom while a storm raged outside? Can you fathom the responsibility of keeping the lantern burning brightly when certain doom faced approaching ships in a blinding storm? The life of a keeper had an air of mystique to it. I find it a romantic era of man and the sea; how those two must have become well acquainted! And I find it somewhat sad that few keepers are needed today since lighthouses are now automated. Somehow knowing an old salty sailor was manning the station to ensure your safety created a personal feeling of protection and welcome concern. Still, lighthouses will ever be cherished because of the light they bring regardless of how the light is delivered.

In 1999, I joined my parents for a week on *Agape* back on Chesapeake Bay. It was a wonderful experience to revisit the beautiful places we had cruised to almost twenty years earlier. We cruised to Tangier Island, Mobjack Bay, the Severn River, and down through Hampton Roads into Norfolk. All along this path my camera was snapping pictures of the lighthouses we passed. The lighthouses of the Chesapeake are among the most beautiful in the world. But my heart took even better pictures. This was especially so on a stormy day when we were at the mouth of Mobjack Bay. The rain was intense, and the wind kicked up five-foot swells. I was excited to have a rugged, salty day to feel like a true sailor once again!

As we looked for the entrance to Mobjack Bay, we studied our navigational charts to identify marked buoys for determining our location. The wind was howling, and the salt spray made it difficult to see. We needed to get into a safe anchorage. And then we saw it: New Point Comfort Lighthouse. Even the *name* of the lighthouse was welcome to see on the chart. The lighthouse marks the entrance to the Bay, but it hasn't been operational since an offshore beacon replaced it in 1963. The light was unlit, but there it stood anyway—a visual landmark to let us know where to head for safe harbor. I thought of how this white lighthouse had guided sailors into this same harbor since 1806 with its black lantern burning brightly.[6] The light no longer shines, but the symbol of a grand history endows this wonderful landmark with bright significance. And this lighthouse still guides sailors in storms, as it did for us.

Back to the Light

Let's get back to the light, the reason we care about lighthouses in the first place. Now that you are a lighthouse trivia buff, how much do you know about light? Our love for light is integral to who we are as humans, and it's where everything began.

Light comprised the first day of creation. "Now the earth was formless and empty, and darkness was over the surface of the deep, and the Spirit of God was hovering over the waters. *(Visualize that!)* And God said, 'Let there be light,' and there was light. God saw that the light was good, and he separated the light from the darkness" (Genesis 1:2–4, NIV).

Light enables us to function and to get things accomplished. God couldn't proceed with the rest of creation until there was light. Not that God can't see in the dark, but He knew that all of creation's existence would be dependent on light. Light gives life to plants, which in turn fuel life on Earth. Plants give life-sustaining oxygen, which all living creatures need. Light provides the world with a 24-hour clock by which to turn from day to day and season to season. Light allows people and animals to function in work, in play, and in daily existence. We can't see in the dark.

Light reveals things hidden in the dark. "The commands of the LORD are radiant, giving light to the eyes" (Psalm 19:8b, NIV). Light reveals truth. Think about the figures of speech we use that mirror this scripture. "Put things in a whole new light." "Shed some light on the subject." Even "We'll leave the light on for ya." Light shows things as they truly are both in a physical sense and a figurative sense. Next time you are in an unfamiliar building, go into a dark room and shut the door. Wait a minute and just think about what could be in there. If you've never been there, you don't know, do you? Uneasy? Now turn on the light switch. *Voila!* That room becomes much more comfortable. You can see everything clearly. Life with God is very much the same.

Since God can see in the darkness of life, and we can't, He gave us "flashlights" of His truth to guide us through. His commands of how to live are meant not to keep us in darkness, but to keep us in the light. Think about that. We were not meant to stumble around, lost in the dark. We were meant to see things clearly and truthfully so we can live abundantly. Truth is like . . . visual oxygen for the soul. Truth is liberating; it sets us free to see things not only as they are, but also as they *can* be when we follow God's lead.

Light guides us along the right path. "Your word is a lamp for my feet, a light on my path" (Psalm 119:105, NIV). Once we have the truth of God's flashlight in our hands, what does that enable us to do? It enables us to move ahead. We no longer must remain in the same place for fear of falling and getting hurt, for fear of getting lost, or for fear of some unknown, imaginary "boogey man." God's word is the light that keeps our path lit. Keep moving! He has much planned for you to see. There's so much waiting for you around the corner—more than you could ever imagine.

Light makes fear recede. "The LORD is my light and my salvation—whom shall I fear?" (Psalm 27:1, NIV). Once you have visual oxygen and a well-lit path, you can see everything that comes your way. Light conquers darkness. Darkness cannot exist when light is around. When you have that kind of power in life, fear evaporates. Fear thrives on the unknown, and it can no longer thrive when exposed by light. This is a crucial aspect of God that He wants you to understand. He is your light and your salvation. We know what light does, but what about salvation? What does salvation mean?

Salvation means you are saved from that which would destroy you. Did you get that? You are saved from *anything* that would seek to bring you down. You are saved first and foremost from death—Jesus provided the ultimate showdown with darkness and won. He knows full well what it's like to be lost in the darkness of death. And He allowed Himself to be consumed by its blackness so we would never have to experience such hopelessness. I can imagine how Jesus must have felt when He saw the first ray of light before His resurrection. Hope, relief, completion, elation. You see, like a lighthouse keeper, Jesus knows by experience the value of a light. Light is a powerful deliverer. Death can't touch you if you remain in the light.

You are saved also from harm. This doesn't mean you won't experience physical hurt or emotional pain in life. What it does mean is that God will not allow more than you can bear, and He will hold you in the palm of His hand when you are in the midst of difficulty. Storms are a part of life. But He will shed light on the situation so you will be able to see that He is clearly protecting you from that which would seek to destroy you.

Salvation means you are saved from the uncertainty that paralyzes your ability to function. God sometimes makes the light shine farther down the path than what is immediately under our feet so we can see a little ahead. Sometimes He makes the light shine only one step ahead, allowing us only to see what we need to see at that moment. But think how perfect that is! He knows when and how much we need to see for every given circumstance. If we see too much ahead, He knows we might become overwhelmed and unwilling to proceed. If we don't see enough, fear might creep into the picture and make us want to retreat. This is a great truth for you wherever you are on the path. Remember, He already *knows* what's out there down your path.

Are you uncertain about your physical condition? Follow the Light. Are you afraid of making the wrong decision about something? Follow the Light. Have you messed up and stumbled in the dark? Follow the Light. Are you totally lost and don't know where to turn? Follow the Light. Do you live in fear of what will happen to you in life? Follow the Light. The Lord is your light and your salvation, so whom in the world should you fear? No one. Nothing. Zip. Nada. Let the fear go and watch it vanish in the light.

Finally, and most importantly, light is embodied in Christ. "In Him was life, and the life was the light of men. And the light shines in the darkness, and the darkness did not comprehend it" (John 1:4-5, NKJV). "When Jesus spoke again to the people, he said, 'I am the light of the world. Whoever follows me will never walk in darkness, but will have the light of life'" (John 8:12, NIV). Did you hear that promise written *just for you*? If you follow Christ, you will never walk in darkness. Your light will never go out. You will live in truth, free from fear and lostness. Take a moment and ponder that. Is that something you want? I sure do. Some people choose to remain in darkness and uncertainty. God gives free choice to all. But there are only two choices: darkness or light. Which one do you choose?

Jesus said that no one goes to the Father except by Him. God is the safe harbor, and Jesus is the lighthouse. No one reaches the safe harbor except by following the guiding beacon of light.

Doesn't it make sense now to understand why we love lighthouses? We are all searching for safety, and we inherently know the way when we see the light. Allow Jesus to be your New Point Comfort in this dark and stormy life. He remains the resident lightkeeper. He will never become automated or leave His post. He is the salty sailor hero . . . who knows by experience the value of a light. He will ever be scanning the horizon for vessels lost at sea and bringing them safely into shore.

One more word association. Ready? "Light," quick! What comes to mind? If you said "Jesus" . . . good answer. You get an A+. Class dismissed.

PART THREE

ROUGH SEAS AND BATTERED SHORES

"An angry sea roars its approach,
gnaws with grey fangs the helpless shore.
Tears at the cliff face–brings it hurtling down to be devoured.
Things man intended to last a thousand years splintered to shards,
ground into sand and anonymity."

—Pam Brown[1]

Some went out on the sea in ships;
they were merchants on the mighty waters.
They saw the works of the Lord, his wonderful deeds in the deep.
For he spoke and stirred up a tempest that lifted high the waves.
They mounted up to the heavens and went down to the depths;
in their peril their courage melted away. They reeled and staggered
like drunkards; they were at their wits' end. Then they cried out to
the Lord in their trouble, and he brought them out of their distress.
He stilled the storm to a whisper; the waves of the sea were hushed.
They were glad when it grew calm,
and he guided them to their desired haven.

—Psalm 107:23–30, NIV

Chapter 8

EVEN THE WIND AND THE WAVES

I wish you were with me here right now. I wish you could feel the tremendous winds that are blowing and see the whitecaps that blanket the Gulf of Mexico. A terrific storm is approaching the shore, and it is announcing its arrival quite well, saying, "Haloo! Here I come!" I'm watching things get blown away. A welcome mat on the stoop of the house next door is now a lawn ornament. Towels, drying on the railing from the warm swim today, are lying on the ground. The empty white rocking chair on the porch here next to me is going to town like God Himself is seated there, giddy with excitement as to what is happening. The sound is incredible! I love the rush of wind that brags of its own sheer power.

I'm looking at the limbs of these wind-blown pine trees that surround the house. They are bending to the will of the wind as they've done for decades. Their twisted branches point to the west from the easterly winds that have blown in countless storms. But there is a funny sight amid this turmoil: two doves sitting as calmly as can be on one of those twisted branches . . . just staring at me. They act as if nothing is amiss. They are grooming themselves and seem to be enjoying just hanging out while their branch sways in the wind. A fierce storm is approaching, but they are not worried in the least. I never thought I could have anything in common with doves, but I do. I share their sentiments exactly.

I love it when the winds howl, and the whitecaps appear. I like to see a good challenge of natural forces combating for victory. The sand and the waves are going at it. The wind and the trees are going at it. And I'm sitting here, calm, cool, and collected with my pals, George and Gracie, the doves. Oooh! Some lightning just lit up the darkened horizon—what a *beaut!* This is cool. I adore storms. My laptop on the other hand is sweating because it is plugged in now. I better take care of that.

Some people hate storms, and some people love them; to each his or her own. BOOM! (Sorry, some thunder just joined in the chorus. The storm must be getting close.) Self-analysis time . . . hmmm . . . why do I love storms?

Well, I love the change that occurs. I love the action. I love the uncertainty as to what is going to happen. I love the sudden drop in temperature that puts a chill up my spine. I love the energy and the noise. And I love the fact that I am safe and secure because I know the storm Producer quite well. I know that God Himself is the Maestro who is conducting this storm. *This* symphony of a storm will receive a standing ovation when it is over.

Ahhh, here comes the rain. Cooling rain, thirst-quenching rain, refreshing rain. A full symphony of sound and motion is now in place. That empty rocking chair next to me is really living up to its name now. Of course, I can say all of this while being calm and cool, because I only have to walk five feet and go inside a snug, safe beach house if it gets too rough out here on the porch. If I were out there on a boat in the gulf riding those whitecaps, I might not be so cool. Why is that? The storm is the same, but my position in the storm is different in those two scenarios.

Riding a boat over waves in turmoil can be disconcerting. It can also be a blast, but it can be disconcerting when the storm is way bigger than you are. And storms can pop up faster than you can anticipate. There is a certain sea that is notorious for sudden storms, and I've sailed on it. I was fortunate enough to have a sunny day to enjoy smooth sailing, but others have not been so fortunate. I'm talking about the Sea of Galilee, and about Jesus' disciples.

One day, Jesus wanted to go out for a sail. But He was just beat from a hard day at the office—healing people, casting out demons, opening thousands of eyes to the glory of God—you know, your typical, regular day job. Anyway, He decided He would go take a nap in the stern of the boat while His disciples sailed around the Sea of Galilee. Suddenly the winds started to blow, and whitecaps blanketed the sea. The joyride turned into a terror ride. The boat began to fill with water, and they were in danger. But Jesus kept on sleeping. He was oblivious to the storm, just like George and Gracie.

Jesus' disciples started crying out, "We're all going to die! Goodbye, cruel world!" Somebody decided that it would be nice to wake Jesus before they capsized and went over and shook His shoulder. Jesus woke up. The disciples cried out their doom and gloom and said they were soon going to be history because of the storm.

Jesus rubbed His eyes, looked at His disciples, and shook His head. He got up, looked at the turbulent sea and said, "Hush! Be quiet! Can't you see I'm trying to get some sleep here?" (Well, those weren't His *exact* words . . .)

An amazing thing happened. Immediately the winds stopped. The whitecaps disappeared, and the sea turned to glass. The sails grew limp and lazily flapped without the winds to keep them full. The disciples stood there with their mouths hanging open. Jesus then turned to His dumbfounded disciples and said, "Where is your faith? Like I didn't know you were in trouble . . . as *if*!" They all looked at each other and said, "Who in the world *is* this guy? He says, 'Hush!' and even the wind and the waves obey Him." It doesn't say so, but I bet Jesus then went back to bed and got some more shut-eye, allowing His disciples to calmly sit and think about what had happened.

Forgive my paraphrase of this passage in Luke 8:22–25, but I hope my animated version of this incredible story allowed you to see *two* storms calmed by Jesus. The first storm was the obvious one: the one with wind and waves. I appreciate an insight from a Bible commentary about this scene.[1] There were times when Jesus decided it would be appropriate to show His power to the disciples. They needed to fully understand that He truly was who He claimed to be as the Son of God. He has ultimate authority over nature and can start or stop a storm with just a word. When the situation merited such a display of power, Jesus used it as a teachable moment. He wisely used such displays sparingly. But the display of His power over the forces of nature drove home the fact that He, indeed, is God.

But there was another storm that Jesus calmed. A storm of fear and despair raged within the hearts of the disciples, and Jesus calmed that storm with the same word, "Hush." Hearts grew still with the calming peace of salvation. The disciples realized that they were not going to die. They were going to live because Jesus said so.

We, too, experience both types of storms, don't we? We experience literal storms like the one I'm watching unfold before me as I write this. I'll take these storms any day. But we also experience emotional storms in life that threaten our peace of mind. Those types of storms I would rather not take . . . any day. The disciples were in the presence of the living God but still felt as if they would drown because of the storm. Their faith is what had actually drowned. But I don't think I can be too hard on them. Don't we all sometimes experience faith drowning when bad life storms come?

I wonder why that is. When we accept Christ into our hearts, we also are in the presence of the living God. But let those life storms suddenly pop up, and we start to whimper and cry out that certain doom is near. We wonder what is happening and why. We think of all the things we have done that could have caused the storm, as if we are being punished. Our hearts and minds become so frantic that we finally think to call out to Jesus, "Hey, I'm dying here, but before I do, I thought I'd give you a heads-up!"

Jesus shakes His head at us, looks at the storm in our hearts, and says, "Hush. Be still." Then He looks at us and asks, "Where is your faith? Like I didn't know you were in trouble." Ouch. Been there, done that too many times to mention. The calm comes, our mouths hang open, our hearts settle, and we ask, "Who *is* this guy?" It seems like we need those displays of His power in our lives as our most teachable moments as well. But this is what I want you to see. With life storms Jesus sometimes quiets the circumstances of the storms, but that is not the aspect of the storm that He is out to still. What He is after is the storm in our hearts. He wants us to be still and know down deep in our hearts that He is God, regardless of what is going on around us.

Storms will always be raging around us in life; that's just a given. What is not a given is the storm within. When He asks us where our faith is, He is talking about our belief in His unmatched ability to protect us mentally, emotionally, and spiritually. Oh sure, He could calm the *circumstances* that are producing the turmoil around us, but God wisely chooses to use such displays of His power sparingly. He respects the freedom of allowing our lives to result from how we choose to live them. He respects the growth that always comes when we have to fight our own battles. Remember the analogy I made earlier about this literal storm raging around me? I love this storm while sitting on the secure porch of my house, but if I were out in a boat, I would be afraid. The storm is the same, but my position in the storm is different.

Well, the analogy with life storms isn't much different. Doesn't our position in the storm determine how we feel about it? If we feel safe and secure from the storm, we can appreciate it and even enjoy it. But if we feel vulnerable and exposed to the elements of destruction, we scream doom and gloom. If our hearts are safe and secure near the haven of Jesus, we can appreciate and maybe (rarely) enjoy life storms because we realize that we will not be harmed. We realize that Jesus can stop the circumstances with a word, but if He chooses not to, we rest in the fact that He will use those circumstances for our good and for our growth. If our hearts are not securely near the haven of Jesus, we feel vulnerable and exposed to the elements of destruction. We just know our ship is going down.

When Jesus asks, "Where is your faith?" He is asking what position you are in for the storm. Are you on the porch, or are you out in the Gulf?

We have an incessant need to be reminded that we are indeed safe from harm. I think the childlike heart in all of us loves that comforting feeling of security and protection from storms. When the winds rage, the waters pound, the lightning strikes, and the thunder booms, we love to run for cover and jump into the arms of our "Abba," our heavenly Father. He will never turn us away but will always hold us tightly until the storm has passed, hushing our stormy emotions. Choose your life storm position wisely—what an incredible difference it makes.

How poignant that the dove symbolizes peace . . . peace amidst the storm. When my next life storm comes, I hope I can be a little more like George and Gracie. Meanwhile, I'll just sit back with them on the porch and enjoy God's orchestration of this beach storm while it lasts. I know that even the wind and the waves will have to eventually stop and obey Him . . . whenever He gives the word.

By faith the people passed through the Red Sea as on dry land; but when the Egyptians tried to do so, they were drowned.

—Hebrews 11:29, NIV

Chapter 9

THE RED SEA

Small Minds

Persecution. Oppression. Back up against the wall. No way out. Put through the ringer. Totally . . . helpless. Ever been there? Have you been in such a valley before? I'd say it would be a challenge to find someone who *hasn't* been there. It starts when you're a toddler, doesn't it? Some other kid steals your toy, knocks you down, and gets *you* in trouble. A little later it's either bullies or gossips at school that inflict persecution by stealing your lunch money, or worse, your self-esteem. Then in the real world, it's the bosses, co-workers, and customers that can wreak havoc by trying to steal your self-identity, trying to bend you to their will with power struggles.

Small minds, all of them. Small minds that never grew up. Small minds lacking in knowledge, wisdom, integrity, and fairness. Small hearts that sadly feel there's no other way to win. But in the end, they always lose.

I've met lots of small people with this "Napoleon syndrome" of having to act big to make others think they *are* big. And I'm sure I'll meet many more in the years to come. Small people are just part of life. But small people do hurt us and can knock us off the mountain when they play king of the hill. We land in the valley after a tumble and feel that we are at our worst.

Ah, but *contraire, mon frère.* Valleys are where it gets good. Valleys are where you grow. Valleys are where you heal, gain strength, wisdom, and a whole new perspective on life. Because if you allow Him to, God will use this valley time to take you to new heights. This is God's favorite place to hang out, because this is where He does His finest work.

The Valley

Let me recount a familiar story for you if you don't mind. Once there was a nation of people enslaved by small-minded yet brilliant rulers. These slaves were forced to build buildings and monuments to establish the empire of the most powerful man in the world, Pharaoh. Conditions were harsh. They were persecuted, oppressed, had their backs up against the wall, and had no way out. They were helpless. They were in a valley of despair, and they cried to God. He heard them, and devised the most ingenious, clever rescue ever conceived.

God chose a man named Moses to be a "mole" in this Egyptian Empire. He worked it in such a way that the very people who sought to kill Moses would end up raising him as one of their beloved sons. Moses' mother was in a dark valley as she put her baby in a basket in the river to save his life. Pharaoh's daughter found Moses floating in the river and fell in love with him. She wanted him for her own and so named him Moses, which means "I drew him out of the water." God was too cool; Pharaoh's daughter needed a nurse for the baby, so he arranged for Moses' own mother to get the job! Do you think Moses' mother soared to the heights on that one? You better believe it.

So, Moses was raised as an Egyptian, and became one of the foremost leaders in the empire. But—this part I love—Moses was a Hebrew. And the slaves were Hebrews, too. Moses finally learned the truth about his true identity, did some not-so-good things, and had to leave town. He went into the desert and decided to stay in Midian. There he met his wife, and God. Moses met God face to burning bush. And God told Moses that he was going to free the Israelites from bondage and lead them out of Egypt. Moses protested, "This is an impossible task, God! I don't want this. WHY ME?!" They talked it out, and Moses reluctantly took the job.

Moses went back to Egypt and told the new Pharaoh, "God says, 'Let my people go.'" Pharaoh said, "No way!" So, Moses had to rough him up with some plagues, compliments of God. Things got much worse in the process. Pharaoh roughed up the slaves even harder. The Israelites became angry with Moses. Here he was doing all he could to save these people by doing exactly what God said to do, and all he saw were matters getting worse. He was doing everything right but was persecuted by those he was working so hard to help. Moses entered a very low valley. His back was against the wall, but still he kept on as God directed him to do.

Eventually, the Angel of Death broke Pharaoh's spirit by taking his firstborn son. Pharaoh told Moses the people could leave, so Moses told everyone to pack up. "We're out of here!" Off they went, free from the bondage and from the small minds that had held them captive for so long.

God then decided to get even more mileage from this experience. He decided to show the Israelites and the Egyptians that He was the true, all-powerful God. He didn't want there to be any doubt from anyone. So, He hardened Pharaoh's heart. Pharaoh then said, "What have I done?! GET MY SLAVES BACK NOW!" Pharaoh and his army of six-hundred chariots pursued the Israelites to bring them back into bondage.

Meanwhile Moses and the Israelites camped out at a lovely spot by the Red Sea. All of a sudden, they looked up, saw the Egyptians coming, and panicked. Moses told the people to be still and wait on God's deliverance. But God said, "Hey, don't just sit there! Move!" Moses must have thought, "Uh, where to, God? The only direction we can move is *into* the Red Sea." God said, "You're absolutely right—not a problem. Take that staff of yours and stretch your hand out over the sea. The water will divide so the Israelites can go through on dry ground. I'll harden the hearts of the Egyptians, and they'll keep right on coming in after you. I'll swallow them up with the sea. Then the Egyptians will know the real Me. They will know that I mean business when I say, 'Don't mess with my children.'"

> Then Moses stretched out his hand over the sea, and all that night the LORD drove the sea back with a strong east wind and turned it into dry land. The waters were divided, and the Israelites went through the sea on dry ground, with a wall of water on their right and on their left. The Egyptians pursued them, and all Pharaoh's horses and chariots and horsemen followed them into the sea. During the last watch of the night the LORD looked down from the pillar of fire and cloud at the Egyptian army and threw it into confusion. He jammed the wheels of their chariots so that they

> had difficulty driving. And the Egyptians said, "Let's get away from the Israelites! The LORD is fighting for them against Egypt."
>
> Then the LORD said to Moses, "Stretch out your hand over the sea so that the waters may flow back over the Egyptians and their chariots and horsemen." Moses stretched out his hand over the sea, and at daybreak the sea went back to its place. The Egyptians were fleeing toward it, and the LORD swept them into the sea. The water flowed back and covered the chariots and horsemen—the entire army of Pharaoh that had followed the Israelites into the sea. Not one of them survived. (Exodus 14:21–28, NIV)

The small minds were no more.

The Mountain

The Israelites caught their breath after that harrowing experience, and then had a party! They praised God and celebrated. What a rescue! But God still had greater plans in mind. He rescued their bodies from slavery—now it was time to rescue their souls for eternity. God directed Moses to go to Mt. Sinai to receive the rescue document: the Ten Commandments. With His own finger, God wrote the laws onto stone tablets that would provide the rescue for His people in how they lived, worshipped, and related to one another. (This was to be the covenant for a time, until Christ brought a new covenant into play.) So, while everyone encamped around the base of Mt. Sinai, Moses left the valley and walked up the mountain. There he met THE King of the Hill. Moses came down from the mountain with the law of God.

The impossible made possible. The helpless turned hopeful. And from his valley, God brought Moses back to the heights.

What a powerful story. It's almost too hard to believe, isn't it? Sometimes Bible stories can seem like fairy tales too good to be true. But it happened. I've been to where it happened, and it is an incredible place. Allow me to share my experience there if I may.

Desert Nomads

We were en route from Jerusalem to Cairo to see the ruins of the mighty empire that God brought down. While traveling there via the Gaza Strip, our route was obstructed by protestors. We ended up having to take an alternate route across the desert. Sand drifts blocked our road, and every now and then, we would have to stop while army bulldozers cleared the way. It was rather exciting; we even made the headlines in *The Jerusalem Post*. After a long day, we got to the Egyptian border and went through customs, but they would not allow us to enter Egypt. Our group visa was not in order, and we were denied entry. We then had to drive all the way back to Tel Aviv and devise another plan. We wanted to see Egypt, and we arranged to do just that. But we didn't see the Egypt of Pharaoh. We saw the Egypt of Moses. There was never a better consolation prize; it was better than the original plan.

The Red Sea

We boarded an incredibly old twin-engine plane and flew to Eilat, a port on the Red Sea. As we flew over the Red Sea, it amazed us to see the red color of the water, and we learned how the Red Sea got its name. The red mountains surrounding the Red Sea reflect onto the surface of the water, making it appear red. The glory of the mountains reflects in the valley of sea below.

I walked out onto a long pier into the Red Sea and went to an underwater viewing area to see all the fish and beautiful marine life in this thriving sea. And I thought to myself, "These creatures had to go somewhere when Moses split the waters." If you've seen the animated movie, *The Prince of Egypt*, the parting of the Red Sea is one of the most remarkable scenes my eyes have ever witnessed. Behind the wall of water on either side, fish and even whales swim in the parted sea, towering stories above the Israelites as they walked through. Think about that! It was the world's first walk-through aquarium.

I can see a terrified child suddenly stop to stand eye to eye with a dolphin. I'm sure that dolphin would have given that child comforting reassurance with its gentle smile. I can see that child reaching into the wall of water to touch the dolphin on its beak, and smile back. I can see that dolphin swim alongside the child within that wall of water until the child is safely across. God is always in the details. He sends comforters to help us along while we walk through our Red Seas.

I was blessed to visit the place where this miracle occurred, and it brought the fairy tale feeling of the story up to a greater reality for me. But we also saw the place where Moses met God, and the reality of *that* encounter left me speechless.

Sinai

We flew in that noisy plane to the middle of the Sinai desert. We landed on an airstrip built especially for the Egyptian President, Anwar Sadat, when he wanted to visit Sinai. At the end of the airstrip was a small building made of plain, white cinderblocks surrounded by a group of Mercedes. I thought it was a mirage. Egypt is full of extreme scenes!

It was time to see Mt. Sinai, but I didn't take a Mercedes—I opted for a camel. I rode this nasty, spitting, smelly animal to the base of Mt. Sinai, but forgot all about the camel when I looked up to see Sinai. There stood this tall, majestic, rocky mountain towering over me. I tried to envision that same child who met the dolphin look up to the top of Mt. Sinai where God Himself encamped. Here he was, this small child in a deep valley. And there HE was—the God who had delivered him here. Little did that child know that his true rescue had only just begun.

Been There. Done That.

It's one thing to read the Bible story of Moses and the Red Sea and appreciate the miracle that occurred. It's another thing to see where it happened. But it's an even greater thing still to experience what it feels like to be rescued by the *very same God* that delivered the Israelites. It's an awesome thing to fall into a valley from small-minded people and be brought back up to heights that make you tower over those small minds. That's the "been there, done that" experience that awaits you, and it is the best experience of them all.

> When I despair, I remember that all through history, the way of truth and love has always won. There have been murderers and tyrants, and for a time they can seem invincible. But in the end they always fall. Think of it, always. —*Mohandas Gandhi*

I've been seriously persecuted by small minds at work twice in my career. The first time, God delivered me from that unstable organization by allowing them to let me go. Of course, I didn't see it as a delivery at the time; it felt more like an exile! Oh, but what a delivery it was, and to the best valley I've ever been to. God was already there waiting for me to arrive. He said, "OK, are you ready to really get to know Me? Are you ready to watch the Master at work? Then be still and watch for a time. And when I give the word, you walk right on through."

For three months, God taught me things about Him through His word that I had never realized. I simply lived in the Psalms, and read them all, repeatedly. I read the experiences of David and was amazed that he felt just like I did. He faced persecution, trials, and valleys, and had the same Deliverer return him to the mountaintop. It was during this time that I spiritually "grew up." God separated the sea of despair for me, and I walked through on dry ground to the other side, a much wiser person. I walked right into the best job anyone could ever want with an even better salary and benefits than what I left behind.

But guess what God did next? He swallowed up my old employer and put the company out of business. As He did with the Egyptians, He said, "Don't mess with My child. Or with Me." The small minds were no more. Vengeance is God's business, not ours.

Years later I walked through another valley of persecution, but this time I had to stay put at the company. This time God showed me how to love my enemy. I stumped my persecutor with kindness and love. Eventually it melted that person's heart, and God used that person to work out my best interests at work. Unfortunately, after God had delivered me safely to the other side of that bad work situation, the person was let go. Once again, God dealt with the small mind that sought to harm me. But even now, years later, I still pray for that person. It's a wild feeling to love your enemy. They *really* lose the power to hurt you; your spirit is set free.

When you are a child of God, you enter into a fiercely protective relationship. God is committed to allowing you to enter valleys in life so you can grow, learn, and mature. But He is also committed to walking you safely through and bringing you back up to the mountaintop. And He takes care of the small minds that hurt you along the way.

He is God, but He cannot be put into a box. God is sovereign, and He chooses the how's, when's, where's, and who's of deliverance. Sometimes

His method of deliverance doesn't appear to be deliverance at all. Sometimes it doesn't make sense, and it does look like the small minds win. What about those who die for their faith? Where is God? I can't give you a reason or an explanation. But this I know: those martyrs are immediately brought to the heights with God. The heights in Heaven tower above the heights on Earth. And those small minds *will* someday have to answer for what they've done to God's children. Remember, vengeance is God's. He knows what He is doing. God happened to answer swiftly and visibly with my two situations, but He may work differently in the future. But He never misses the mark when doing His best work.

Of course, His finest work happened when Jesus became *the* King of the Hill. It was all such a paradox: Jesus looked like the persecuted loser. He forcefully climbed the hill of Calvary at the edict of small minds, but they had played right into God's hands. He used small minds to bring about the ultimate rescue for you and for me. The only way out for Jesus was to walk through the valley of death, so that's what He did. He died, and it looked like those small minds had won. Ah but *contraire, mon frère.* Three days later they were the clear losers when Jesus rose from the grave in victory over death!

Your Red Sea

Moses couldn't get to Sinai until he had crossed the Red Sea.

What is *your* Red Sea that you need parted? Does it look impossible to cross, with the small-minded army in pursuit? Do you want deliverance? Do you want to scale the mountaintop with the true King of the Hill? OK, just say so. God is rarin' to go. He can't wait to let you see the Master at work. He wants to teach you things. He wants to heal your heart. He wants to expand your horizons and your mind. Most of all, He doesn't want you to suffer from a small mind, so that's what valleys are for.

He remains the true King of the Hill, the King of the Valleys, and the Supreme Admiral of the Sea. He'll part your Red Sea so you can go to the mountain again. But for now, welcome your time in the valley. As someone once said, the God on the mountain is still God in the valley.

As for you, you were dead in your transgressions and sins, in which you used to live when you followed the ways of this world and of the ruler of the kingdom of the air, the spirit who is now at work in those who are disobedient. . . . But because of his great love for us, God, who is rich in mercy, made us alive with Christ even when we were dead in transgressions—it is by grace you have been saved.

—Ephesians 2:1–2, 4–5, NIV

Chapter 10

THE DEAD SEA

Deadly Waters

Are you familiar with the Dead Sea? It is a magnificent body of water in Israel. Do you know why the Dead Sea is dead? It has numerous inflows of water, but no outflow. Water comes in but nothing goes out. Water sits, evaporates, and leaves behind a mix of salt and minerals that prevents any habitation of life. A fascinating thing about the Dead Sea is that its saltiness provides incredible buoyancy. When I stood on the shore of the Dead Sea, it was amusing to see all the people who went in for a dip to float and feel weightless.

It may make you feel weightless, but the Dead Sea is dead to life. It receives much, but because it does not allow what it receives to move through and change its makeup it is dead to what it could have. The Dead Sea could be a thriving, living sea filled with rich marine life, if only it had an outlet. If only it allowed the life-giving inflow to do its work, it could come alive, and would have to change its name.

Let's think about this for a minute. Death comes when that which is living does not function as it should. Take our bodies, for example. If you consider every conceivable way we can die, whether it be from disease, injury, or cessation of vital organ function, death results from lack of a normal flow of operations. The heart stops beating, and the flow of blood throughout the body stops. The brain stops working, and the flow of instructional nerve impulses stops. The lungs stop breathing, and the flow of life-sustaining oxygen is lost.

The Dead Sea and our bodies don't have much of a say in the matter. There are just some things in the physical realm that we are unable to affect. But not so in the spiritual realm.

The Dead Soul

This premise of the reason for death—that which fails to work as it should—also holds true in the spiritual realm. But this is one area of our lives where we have a choice. We can choose to make things work as they should and have living, vibrant souls . . . or we can choose to stop the flow and have dead souls.

What do I mean by a dead soul? Well, a soul can be dead in two ways. A soul can be dead on an eternal basis with no hope for everlasting life. And a soul can be dead on a temporary basis when things emotionally don't work as they should.

Every Man Is an Island

When it comes to living in our world, the old adage is right: no man is an island. But when it comes to our eternal destiny, *every* man is an island. Every man is separated from that which gives life, God, due to his sin. We're born as sinful islands, separated by a sea of despair.

Sitting in the middle of San Francisco Bay is the infamous Alcatraz, "The Rock," or "Hellcatraz," as it was also called. From 1934 to 1963, Alcatraz was the federal penitentiary where the worst of the worst were confined. Murderers, felons, bank robbers, kidnappers; the toughest, meanest, most notorious gangsters of all time were inmates here. Al "Scarface" Capone, George "Machine Gun" Kelly, and Robert Stroud, "The Birdman of Alcatraz," were among the most famous criminals to inhabit the island. According to an historical account of this terrible place, "Used as a threat against convicts in other federal penitentiaries, Alcatraz took only criminals who couldn't follow rules elsewhere and subjected them to a regimen meant to control their rebellious ways and crush their resistance."[1]

On a recent trip to San Francisco, I decided to tour Alcatraz and see what it was all about. On the boat ride over I was snapping pictures of the beautiful sailboats clipping past on that brisk bay breeze. Our sailboat, *Agape*, was built near to here, and was actually designed to sail the waters of San Francisco Bay. How I wished for her here so I could test her design. The spectacular Golden Gate Bridge stood majestically in the distance. The blue water was brilliant with the sun's reflection. I thought to myself on the way over to the island, "Well, if you had to go to prison, what a beautiful place to be. I mean, look at this incredible scenery. These prisoners had it made with the view anyway." Was I ever wrong; looks can be deceiving.

As I walked through the cell house down the corridors lined with five-by-nine-foot cells, an incredible oppression came over me. I investigated Al Capone's cell and wondered how this man must have felt. He came to Alcatraz a powerful, murderous criminal who let nothing stand in his way; he left a broken man with nothing. I stepped inside "the hole" which was a cell used for solitary confinement where disobedient prisoners were left to contemplate their behavior in total darkness. I walked into the dining hall where riots occurred, and where men were killed. I heard the stories of riots, failed breakout attempts, suicides, and the infamous breakout by Frank Morris and brothers Clarence and John Anglin, made famous by the *Escape from Alcatraz* movie. I saw those three cells where those three men dug their way to freedom to escape along the roof and into the Bay. They were never found; whether they died or not, they did gain freedom, from Alcatraz, at least.

But the most poignant thing I saw was a corridor with two small windows overlooking the Bay and the Golden Gate Bridge. Except for these small windows, barbed wire or bars hindered every view at Alcatraz. It was also here that the sounds of life could be heard, carried along on that brisk bay wind and behind the bars into the prison. The inmates could faintly hear music, laughter, and women's voices. The haunting sounds were always loudest on New Year's Eve. The inmates sought after this spot in the cell house just so they could stand to see a clear view and hear signs of life. But the sights and sounds, however welcome to break the isolation and monotony, only added to their despair. A former prisoner called it "an island of the living dead."[2] I heard the voice of a former prisoner on my headset explain why I was so wrong in my assumption that the prisoners were fortunate to be on such a scenic island. He said, "Here we were in this harsh place, and all we could see outside was what we were missing. We saw the life going on around us that we could have had. And it was all so close to us, just within our reach."

That is what I mean by a dead soul.

These men were dead eternally as we all are, without the intervening grace of God. On the eternal scale of things, I am no better than Al

Capone. I fall short. You fall short. There is no way to get off our island of death except through grace.

> As for you, you were dead in your transgressions and sins, in which you used to live when you followed the ways of this world and of the ruler of the kingdom of the air, the spirit who is now at work in those who are disobedient. . . . But because of his great love for us, God who is rich in mercy, made us alive with Christ even when we were dead in transgression—it is by grace you have been saved. (Ephesians 2:1–2, 4–5, NIV)

There is only one way to make things work eternally as they should. And that is to simply accept the grace you have already been given. There is nothing you can do to earn it. The only thing you need to do is accept it. But too often we struggle, plan our escape, and try to dig and work our way off our island, driven by hopelessness and a thirst for peace. Do you know what grace is? Many definitions exist to help us grasp the meaning of this incredible gift, but my pastor friend, Dr. Jim Johnson, found and shared the best one I've ever heard, especially for this prison analogy. It goes like this: "Justice is getting what you deserve. Mercy is *not* getting what you deserve. Grace is getting what you *don't* deserve." Wow. The inmates of Alcatraz received justice. Isn't that what we deserve as well?

Jesus chose to uphold justice by paying the sentence Himself. His intense love and compassion for us moved Him to give us not just mercy, but grace. We are the worst of the worst, but Jesus is the best of the best, and gave us our eternal pardon. Escape from our island of death is easy, but it was costly.

On the temporary scale of things in our everyday lives we have the latitude in determining the condition of our souls. The choices we make, the actions we take, the way we relate to others: all of these things determine if our souls are alive from working as they should, or dead from stopping the flow of life-giving hope. The inmates of Alcatraz chose to stop the flow of that which was good into their lives, and they certainly stopped the outward flow of goodness. They were born into freedom with a precious life to live and a country abounding in opportunity in which to live it.

But they killed, they robbed, they broke the law, and stopped the flow. Rule 5 in "Regulations for Inmates" read, "You are entitled to food, clothing, shelter, and medical attention. Anything else you get is a privilege."[3]

Most of us aren't hardened criminals, but the principle remains the same. We have the same freedom of choice. What about in our relationships? Say you are in a romantic relationship, and all you do is receive an inflow of love from another individual, yet there is no outflow from you. What do you suppose will happen to that relationship? It will be a Dead Sea of love. If you amass wealth or possessions, yet disallow even a trickle to go out to share with others, what do you suppose will happen to your satisfaction with all of your "stuff"? It will be a Dead Sea of happiness. What if you gain degree after degree of knowledge, yet never once use that knowledge for anything? What do you suppose will happen to that education? It will be a Dead Sea of intellect. Let's make it harder. What if you go to church, read your Bible, listen to Christian music, but never allow the inflows of such grace to flow out of you as a changed individual? What do you suppose will happen to your faith? It will be a Dead Sea of spirituality.

Do you see how a dead soul can form? If we don't allow grace to permeate us on inflow *and* outflow—eternally and temporally—we are dead in the water. But here's the great news! Dead is a choice, and one we don't have to settle for. Jesus came to give us options. He came to give us not only life (eternity) but to give us life more abundantly (temporally). Wow! That makes me feel like a free bird. A living, breathing, vibrant sea is there for the taking. Why? Because God hates death and loves us so. How He ever could choose to pardon me and put up with me, I'll never know. But He does, so I'll take it.

Please don't choose to live your life on an island of death, seeing what you could have had. Accept your pardon. Then let the mighty waters of grace flow in and out of you. Once you grasp the powerful stream of God's grace flowing into your life, you will want to break down every possible dam and outflow barrier you have.

But because of His great love for YOU, God who is rich in mercy, made YOU alive with Christ even when YOU were dead in transgression—it is by grace YOU have been saved.

So, there's your sentence. You've been given LIFE.

This embattled shore, portal of freedom,
is forever hallowed by the ideals, the valor,
and the sacrifices of our fellow countrymen.
—Inscription, American Cemetery, Normandy, France

Chapter 11

THE LONGEST DAYS

"Men whose wisdom and courage
make them worthy of heaven are called heroes."

—Motto, Clan Maitland

The Exception

There are times in life when we find exceptions to the rule. True exceptions are not made on a whim to give preferential treatment. True exceptions are so called because of their unusual nature. They rise above the standards by which most abide. True exceptions elevate the playing field. Since the rest of the standards cannot achieve such elevated status, true exceptions are put in a league all their own.

I write about beaches and oceans around the world, with a loving, free-spirited, and sometimes humorous approach. I describe the beach as a place of solace and escape . . . a place of renewal and peace. But I now must make a true exception. There is a coastline of beaches that became the exception on one day. These beaches became exceptional not because of the joy they give, but because of the pain they felt. These beaches were in one day forever removed from my list of beaches for solace and enjoyment. They were forever placed on a sacred list of beaches to grieve, to mourn, and to remember. For me, these beaches are no longer suitable for playful frolic—they are forever only suitable for tearful reflection.

One day—the longest day—changed this coast forever. What happened on this coast changed millions of lives and the course of history. The day—June 6, 1944. The coast—Utah, Omaha, Gold, Sword, Juno—the beaches of D-Day in Normandy, France.

Yesterday, Today, and Tomorrow

1944.

It seems so long ago, but it wasn't, really. I was blessed to be in Normandy for the 57th anniversary of D-Day. I attended the memorial services at Omaha and Utah. I met the brave men who were there that day. I walked through row on row of 9,000 white crosses and stars, sobbing as I read the names of the men who were also there that day, but never went home. I walked through fields lined with hedgerows where paratroopers dropped, and gliders crashed into a night filled with enemy fire. I climbed on top of the Atlantic wall and stood inside the German bunkers from which the hellish fury of destruction was released on those men. And I walked the beaches where it all happened.

The emotions I felt were indescribable. I lived that week with a continual lump in my throat and tears in my eyes. For you see, the realization of what happened in this sacred place is overwhelming. When you grasp not only what happened here—the terrible cost that was paid—but also the implications for our world and its liberation from sheer evil, you touch history. And that history touches you. Time becomes meaningless, for the events transcend the calendar. The events of that longest day in 1944 stretch from the bloody beaches of Normandy all the way into your daily life today. For if D-Day had not occurred, the liberation of Europe from Hitler's grip would not have been achieved. And without the liberation of Europe, freedom on North American shores would have been next in line.

My generation has lived in a wonderful era of peace, knowing truly little war, and knowing *nothing* of what it was like in World War II. I must admit that my generation has also known very little about the events of that terrible time. When I studied modern history in school, the events of WWII did not sink in because of the little time devoted to it in the curriculum. I did not grasp what it was all about until I began studying the war as an adult. When I finally understood what happened, I understood why I am free today, and the gratitude I feel cannot be put into words. I have grown up in a free nation, and in a peaceful time. This is the end result of what the men of WWII wished for their children and their grandchildren. I'm part of those "future generations" for whom the heroes of WWII fought. And it is my heartfelt desire to express my gratitude through my words and through the education of my son; may he know and understand what was done for him by these brave men. May no generation ever say, "That happened so long ago, it's not relevant to me." As long as there is breath in your body, it's relevant for you and for me.

I am grateful for the work of the late Mr. Stephen Ambrose, D-Day historian and author of the fine book *D-Day.* I would like to share excerpts from his book to set the stage of understanding for this chapter. My intent is not to retell the story, but to pay tribute to the men who served and to make some striking spiritual analogies that have gripped my heart.

Yesterday

Operation Overlord was the name of the mission—the mission that France and all of Europe had prayed would bring liberation from German occupation. The sheer planning of the mission was mind-boggling, involving the great minds and industrial strength of nations united to bring Hitler down. It is difficult to conceive of all that was transported across the skies and waters of the English Channel in one 24-hour day. 175,000 soldiers laden with equipment and 50,000 vehicles were flown in by nearly 11,000 airplanes or transported across rough seas in 5,333 ships or watercraft.

Ambrose remarks that with all the ingenuity, planning, manpower, and physical might of the Allies in Operation Overlord, the success or failure of the mission was dependent on a small number of men in the lower ranks of the armed forces. "It all came down to a bunch of eighteen-to-twenty-eight-year-olds. They were magnificently trained and equipped and supported, but only a few of them had ever been in combat. Only a few had ever killed or seen a buddy killed. They were citizen soldiers, not professionals.

"None of them wanted to be part of another war. They wanted to be throwing baseballs, not hand grenades, shooting .22s at rabbits, not M-1s at other young men. But when the test came, when freedom had to be fought for or abandoned, they fought. They were soldiers of democracy. They were the men of D-Day, and to them we owe our freedom."[1]

D-Day began with three words spoken by General Eisenhower, "OK, let's go." Two years of planning and preparations were set in motion by the words of the supreme commander. But it was the enemy commander, General Rommel, who labeled what this day would be like. He set the fortifications in place when building his formidable Atlantic Wall, and he knew what was to come. He would throw all the power of the German army at the Allies as they landed, and he knew what a bloodbath it would be. He knew it would be "the longest day."

Heaven was flooded with prayers as the men embarked for Normandy. Admiral Ramsay noted in his journal, "We shall require all the help that God can give us, and I cannot believe that this will not be forthcoming."[2]

> "Jesus Christ is the same yesterday, today, and forever" (Hebrews 13:8, NLT).

Not only was Heaven flooded with prayers, but I also believe Jesus was there Himself that day. Jesus tended to walk along the beach during pivotal moments in the lives of His children. He had already experienced the pain and loss of the soldiers of D-Day—on His longest day 2,000 years before. Like Eisenhower and Rommel, Jesus knew what was coming.

He knew what was coming but has allowed the free will of His creation to shape the course of history. The good and the evil make polarized choices, and battle is inevitable. Because of his sinful nature, man will always be at war. And freedom is costly. Hitler's freedom of choice exacted an unspeakable price—the loss of life and the enslavement of so many had to be stopped. The freedom of choice of the Allies resulted in their willingness to sacrifice the good to triumph over evil.

On Jesus' longest day, He experienced all of D-Day Himself, for that is what His sacrifice was all about—the triumph of evil meant experiencing it firsthand. He felt every bullet, every wound, every scream, every death, and every telegram. This was part of the process of taking on the sin of the world.

You see He not only felt our sin, but the *effects* of our sin. I do not believe that war itself is sin—it is the result of sin and evil desire, and it ensnares innocents on both sides of the conflict. Yes, Germany was the enemy, but understand that not all Germans agreed with Hitler's regime.

On the other side of those bunkers were many young, terrified men who also didn't want to be there but had to follow orders. The grief of their families was doubled. Not only did those German families lose sons, but they lost sons fighting for an evil cause, and the shame of that was unbearable. Jesus fought and won this battle of good vs. evil, so He knew . . . He knew.

The longest day began in the middle of the night with paratroopers jumping in to secure the beach exit routes, followed by gliders filled with reinforcements. But things went wrong. Troopers were not dropped according to plan and landed in disarray. Gliders were torn apart from enemy fire or from crashing into the impenetrable hedgerows. These men came down in hostile territory right on top of the enemy, and hundreds of them never made it to the ground alive. Pvt. John Fitzgerald of the 502nd, PIR, saw troopers hanging in trees. "Their blood was dripping on this place they came to free."[3] Jesus could relate.

I can envision Jesus in the town square and fields of Sainte-Mère-Église as each paratrooper jumped out into the hellish fury of the night. I can see Him standing with open arms on the ground to catch a soldier shot on his way down, enveloping him with loving arms, saying, "I've got you. I remember that bullet and know your pain, but now you're free from the pain. Let's go home."

I can see Jesus climb through a hedgerow thick with thorns to release a fallen soldier from the snare. "I felt that crash, and I know about the grip of thorns. But you're free from them now—let's go home."

As the armada of ships and naval vessels crossed the English Channel, a group on the deck of the *Bayfield* sang *The Battle Hymn of the Republic* and *Onward Christian Soldiers.* Lt. John Robert Lewis recounts, "This was a very sobering time to sing the words, 'As God died to make men holy, let us die to make men free.'"[4] Jesus could relate.

I can see Jesus at H-hour, 6:30 a.m., on the beach, as the fury of all hell broke loose on the shore. I can see Him in the water as a Higgins boat full of seasick, terrified soldiers makes its way to shore under intense gunfire. Soldiers jump into the water, and some go under. Under the waves I can see Jesus grab a drowning soldier, filling his spirit with the sweet air of eternal life, saying, "I've got you—you can breathe now. I know how you feel. I drowned, too, on the cross. Let's go home."

Farther up on the sand, I can see Jesus catching a fallen soldier, cut down by fire, all the while crying for his mother, "Mother! Help me! Mom!" Jesus gathered that dying soldier in His arms saying, "I've got you. I understand. I called out to my parent, too, when my life was slipping away, and I was full of despair. But I'm here—let's go home."

I can see Jesus commanding an army of angels to minister to the fallen and wounded. I can see Him directing the medics where to go and how to help.

I can see Jesus huddled in a group of disoriented and dismayed officers, trying to figure out what had gone wrong and what to do next. I can see Him bring a verse to the memory of a God-fearing soldier, "I will instruct you and teach you in the way you should go: I will guide you with My eye" (Psalm 32:8, NIV). "Do not be afraid or discouraged because of this vast army. For the battle is not yours, but God's" (2 Chronicles 10:15, NIV). Inexplicable courage and clarity of next steps explode as loudly as the mortars surrounding the men.

Can you imagine the unseen things that happened that day? Thousands of souls left their bodies behind in Normandy. While a visible war was raging, an invisible war of good and evil was raging as well. Were the events of Jesus' longest day on the cross relevant to the soldiers of D-Day? Absolutely. The events of Jesus' bloody day transcended time and reached the bloody beaches of Normandy. This was true not only in what was unseen that day, but in what *was* seen.

Consider the symbol of the cross. There were many crosses on the beach that day. What was on the helmet of a medic attending to the wounded and dying? A cross. What was on the helmet of a clergyman, praying with and ministering to the wounded and dying? A cross. And what marks the graves of thousands of men who died that day and lay buried in Normandy? A cross.

The symbol of the cross meant healing and hope for the wounded, and eternal healing and hope for the dead. Think about it—a device used to inflict the most excruciating death imaginable was and is used to give us healing and hope. Why? Because something happened on that cross on a longest day 2,000 years ago that changed billions of lives and the course of history . . . and the course of eternity.

Today

"D-Day? Oh, I hear it was an incredible battle, but that happened so long ago. It's not relevant to my life today."

"Jesus? Oh, He was good and all, but that happened so long ago. He's not relevant to me today."

Oh, really? Get in a car and drive through your town—you have the freedom to do that. Count how many crosses you see. You'll see them on hospitals where you are free to seek care. You'll see them on churches where you are free to worship. You'll see them on charities where you are free to give. You'll see them around the necks of hundreds of people who are free to wear them. Think of the relevance of the men of D-Day and the freedom they preserved for you and me. Think of the relevance of Jesus' longest day for the men of D-Day. Then think of the relevance of Jesus' longest day for you today. As the men of D-Day liberated Europe, so too did Christ liberate all of mankind.

Longest days are exceptional and life changing. We must never forget:

> Here rests in honored glory a comrade in arms known but to God. —*Inscription on the crosses of unknown soldiers, American Cemetery, Normandy, France*

> But if you suffer for doing good and you endure it, this is commendable before God. To this you were called, because Christ suffered for you, leaving you an example, that you should follow in his steps. . . . "He himself bore our sins" in his body on the cross, so that we might die to sins and live for righteousness; by his wounds you have been healed. (1 Peter 2:20–21, 24, NIV)

> The officers and men of the 6th Naval beach battalion dedicate this plaque to our fallen comrades who gave their lives in defense of good over evil. They are the silent sentinels who from their final resting place above the cliff they perpetually watch over the sacred ground of Omaha Beach. —*Plaque, Omaha Beach monument, June 6, 2001*

> For, "Whoever would love life and see good days must keep his tongue from evil and his lips from deceitful speech. They must turn from evil and do good; they must seek peace and pursue it. For the eyes of the Lord are on the righteous and his ears are attentive to their prayer, but the face of the Lord is against those who do evil." (1 Peter 3:10–12, NIV)

> In honor of the 144 valiant men of Company A, 505th parachute infantry regiment whose exact D-Day mission was to seize La Fière Bridge and prevent enemy crossing easterly. Despite heavy losses, Co. A stood fast. No armed enemy ever crossed this bridge. Never forget them. —*Plaque, La Fière Bridge*

> Be alert and of sober mind. Your enemy the devil prowls around like a roaring lion looking for someone to devour. Resist him, standing firm in the faith, because you know that the family of believers throughout the world is undergoing the same kind of sufferings. And the God of all grace, who called you to his eternal glory in Christ, after you have suffered a little while, will himself restore you and make you strong, firm and steadfast. (1 Peter 5:8–10, NIV)

I am so thankful for the numerous plaques and markers I read along the sights in Normandy. Those words are invaluable to preserving the memory of D-Day. But I also encountered a natural memorial as well. The rocks I picked up on Omaha beach are red. It is as if nature itself cries out, "Remember what happened here! Remember the precious blood that was shed in this place. Remember that the waters breaking on this shore once were red with the lifeblood of heroes."

Tomorrow

Jesus is the same yesterday, today, and tomorrow. But guess what? So is evil. We must always remember so we will be ready for tomorrow.

We must remember what the soldiers of D-Day and WWII stopped, because the very same evil will try to rise up again in the future. Evil transcends time just as the good of Christ does. The supreme commanders of good and evil remain the same across time, and the entire world is subject to battle.

I opened this chapter with the motto of clan Maitland, of which I am a part. Our clan descended from the Mautelents of Normandy, and one of those Mautelents was a knight who fought on those same shores of Normandy almost a thousand years ago. He left those shores to cross the English Channel to fight with William the Conqueror at the Battle of Hastings in 1066. Walking along the beaches of Normandy, I was struck with the irony of war and time. War and battle are nothing new— yesterday, today, or tomorrow—they will always come to the same shores again and again.

In the church of Sainte-Mère-Église are two unique stained-glass windows that were dedicated to the paratroopers of the 82nd American Airborne on the 25th anniversary of D-Day. Embedded in the beauty of colored glass are paratroopers and the symbols of the liberation they brought to Sainte-Mère-Église, France, and all of Europe. One of the windows depicts a winged knight, in full armor, ready for battle. Alongside the knight is the motto of the 82nd: "Ready." That is a motto we all should adopt.

> Finally, be strong in the Lord and in his mighty power. Put on the full armor of God, so that you can take your stand against the devil's schemes. For our struggle is not against flesh and blood, but against the rulers, against the authorities, against the powers of this dark world and against the spiritual forces of evil in the heavenly realms. Therefore, put on the full armor of God, so that when the day of evil comes, you may be able to stand your ground, and after you have done everything, to stand. (Ephesians 6:10–13, NIV)

We must be ready for earthly battle to keep history from repeating itself. But we also must be ready for tomorrow's spiritual battle. And there is one set of armor that is required for both. The armor is truth, righteousness, readiness from the gospel of peace, faith, salvation, and the word of God. We must pray and be alert.

La Prix de la Liberté

The price of liberty. Let me ask you something. Did the men of D-Day sacrifice themselves because you and I had earned it and deserved it? No. Many of us weren't even born yet. Even so, those men realized how precious and valuable we were. Liberation is not dependent on the action of the imprisoned—it is dependent on the *value* of the imprisoned in the eyes of the liberator.

The imprisoned people in Europe were valuable beyond measure. But it wasn't just the people who were imprisoned under tyrannical rule; freedom herself had been taken captive. It was *that* imprisonment that was threatening to cross the English Channel . . . and to cross the Atlantic. Freedom herself had to be liberated, because of the immeasurable value she holds.

With what I imagine were similar words to those of Eisenhower, God launched the liberation of humanity when He said, "OK, let's go." Christ came and liberated our souls, but He also liberated our freedom of choice. Without a price paid for sin, judgment was a done deal—there were no choices. We would have remained imprisoned to death for eternity. Jesus liberated our choice to choose by making the necessary sacrifice. I talk a lot about choice and our eternity because that is how God designed it. He is not a tyrannical ruler but a loving Father who wills you to choose Him . . . so He can take you home when *your* longest day comes.

The End of the Longest Day

> One soldier who did not forget to thank God was Lt. Richard Winters, 506th, PIR, 101st Airborne. At 0001 on June 6, he had been in a C-47 headed to Normandy. He had prayed the whole way over, prayed to live through the day, prayed that he wouldn't fail. He didn't fail. He won the DSC (Distinguished Service Cross) that morning.
>
> At 2400 on June 6, before bedding down at Ste.-Marie-du-Mont, Winters (as he later wrote in his diary), "did not forget to get on my knees and thank God for helping me to live through this day and ask for His help on D plus one."[5]

I can't give you an explanation as to why Lieutenant Winters made it through D-Day and others did not. We each will have our day, and only God knows when that will be. But it is my hope that you, too, will pray to God for deliverance and that you will thank Him for what He has done for you. May you never forget, allowing the events of Jesus' longest day to transcend time and touch you where you are. When *your* longest day comes, may He be able to envelop you in His loving arms and say, "I've got you. Let's go home."

The LORD *replied,*
"Is it right for you to be angry about this?"
—Jonah 4:4, NLT

Chapter 12

ANGRY SEAS

Days of Infamy

I haven't written a word in weeks. A force that I have never experienced at this magnitude has consumed my mind and my spirit. My thoughts are preoccupied with it. My emotions are dominated by it. I haven't been myself lately. I've been a thirsty monster in search of something I can't quite identify to quench this dehydrating thirst.

I should be in Pearl Harbor today, right now, this moment. Instead, I'm sitting here on the beach at sunrise at St. George Island, Florida, drinking coffee . . . feeling a relief in my spirit that I haven't felt in weeks. I'm taking deep breaths of salt air. I'm watching a flock of pelicans fly over the shimmering water. I'm listening to the gentle roll of the surf that rocked me to sleep last night through the open windows in my bedroom. I'm feeling a little bit like my old self. What a relief to see some normalcy for a change! Sea life continues its same rhythm despite what happens in the rest of the world. It feels good to my spirit, but my thoughts turn back to reality, and I am reminded of why I'm here, and not in Pearl Harbor.

So, I get up and go for a bike ride to clear my head. I ride down the familiar paths I've known for ten years on this island of refuge. Surely, things will be as they were here before that day seven weeks ago. But they aren't. Instead of windsocks and banners adorned with pink flamingoes or fish, I see American flags. Even on top of beach houses under construction, American flags flying high in the sea breeze from open rafters. That familiar lump returns to my throat, and tears quicken in my eyes. Although the natural island dwellers haven't changed, the people have.

The gravity of recent events has touched every American. No one has been immune to these feelings with which I struggle. Some may feel them with less or greater intensity than I, but they feel them, nonetheless.

I try to imagine what today would have felt like seeing Pearl Harbor. If I had been there before the events of September 11th, things would have been different, I'm sure. I would have had to imagine how our nation felt when it was maliciously attacked on December 7, 1941. My heart would be saddened, my grief in gazing at the underwater grave of the Arizona would be real, but I would not have been able to fully understand and appreciate what Americans in 1941 felt on that day. I do now. I clearly understand how it feels to have our nation attacked because I saw it happen, along with millions of other Americans.

They say everything changed on that day when planes crashed into the World Trade Center towers and into the Pentagon. It did. Our way of life has changed. Our unity as a country changed. Our complacency about a great many things changed. Our hearts changed. Our futures changed. Our lives changed. And for nearly 3,000 families, their very existence changed. I'm not in Pearl Harbor today due to terrorist threats, but the loss of a trip is nothing in the scheme of things.

There are wives who woke up only to glance at a vacant pillow next to them. There are fathers who are struggling to put bowls of Cheerios on the table while dressing the kids and getting their backpacks ready for school because mothers are no longer there to help. There are children who cling tightly to teddy bears as they cry themselves to sleep in beds that are strange to them because no one is back at home to care for them.

The very thing that makes this country great was attacked. I had no idea that when I wrote "The Longest Days" we'd be at war shortly thereafter. I said to be ready because the very same evil would rise up again. And it has.

I was able to grieve about Normandy and World War II and move on because I knew how it ended. The good guys won. And deep down I know how this war will end—the good guys will win again. But there is much to endure before that end is realized. There are life changes to endure. The pain and loss of war to endure. Emotions to endure. Anger to endure . . . and to get beyond.

A category 4 hurricane is churning down off the Florida Keys today. While the seas here are beautiful and calm, the seas down there are angry. Those seas are hell-bent on having their way and blowing wildly until there is no steam left in them. Nothing can stop it. People might be hurt, and property might be destroyed, but those angry seas will churn anyway. Before you get angry over this, you need to understand something about hurricanes. They are necessary. They are vital to equalizing water temperatures around the globe. So even though they can bring harm, angry seas are vital to keep balance in the earth.

Anger stirs our emotions and heightens our sensitivities to those things most important and vital in life. Without anger, we'd become desensitized to a great many things; complacent to let those things rob us blind.

What about this angry sea in me? What about this monster that is churning my thoughts and my emotions into a fury? Can my anger have a good side to it, like a hurricane? I think the answer is "yes." God created everything about us, including our set of emotions. Anger is one of those emotions. Jesus himself got angry when He cleared the temple of the moneychangers. Since He never sinned, His anger must have served a positive purpose.

I've spent many hours contemplating this emotion of anger, and I've come to my own definition of what it is. Ready for the Cote definition? Anger is the clear result of an endangered or harmed belief, person, place, or thing for which one has a passion. Anger always stems from the endangerment or harm of that which we love. Think about that. Try to recount every time you've been angry and see if that hypothesis holds true. If you can identify another stimulus for anger, I'd love to hear it. If our bodies experience hurt inflicted by others or even from our own doing, we get angry. If our minds experience hurt from confusion or a gnawing lack of understanding, we get angry. If our emotions experience a plethora of possible hurts caused by others or our own internal shortcomings, we get angry. Allow these hurtful things to happen to those we love, and the anger is multiplied.

Anger is a natural human reflex. It stimulates our bodies, minds, and emotions as no other emotion can. It demands an immediate response, and it is never disappointed. We yell, we cry out in a rage, we hit something, we just can't sit still . . . or we are deathly silent as our blood pressure rises.

But guess who designed our emotions? God. Guess who also gets angry? God. Guess who said it's OK to get angry? God. But guess who put a quid pro quo in that emotional equation? God. "Be angry, and do not sin" (Psalm 4:4, NKJV). That makes me so mad. OOPS—sorry, but at least I am being honest. How is it even possible to be angry and not sin? I've had to wrestle with this very question for months now. I've joined the rest of my countrymen on a roller coaster ride of emotions ever since 9/11.

Had I been alive when Pearl Harbor was bombed, I would've been the first to volunteer for the Doolittle Raid so I could bomb Japan right back. I *was* alive when the World Trade Center towers and the Pentagon were bombed, and my first impulse was to volunteer to hit the nuke button to obliterate those responsible. The rage I felt was indescribable. The thoughts I thought were unspeakable. The physical side effects I felt left me with a racing pulse, a dull headache, and a sick feeling in my gut.

How dare someone attack and kill my countrymen?! How dare someone attack my freedom and my way of life?! How dare someone do such horrific things "in the name of God?!" Of *course,* those who did this should die, and die some of them did. I felt no remorse for the hijackers who crashed those planes. I felt an eerie satisfaction. But as Walt Weckler once said, "Revenge has no more quenching effect on emotions than salt water has on thirst."[1]

So, because of the angry seas on which I'm tossed, my spirit has been locked up and immobilized. The patriot in me and the Christian in me have been at war—not that the two are mutually exclusive—they aren't. But my thirst for revenge and retaliation has been unquenched by the concept of grace and forgiveness. Oh, I believe justice is right and true and biblical in nature. But I've been craving more than justice, and that's where my anger has gone over the line. How can I forgive *this?* How can I bestow grace to this true infidel, this evil personified? Well, ultimately, I can't. Only God can. What I must be willing to do is to acknowledge that God's love for those people is just as great as His love for me. And that is what I have not been able to swallow.

It's Christmas now. A season of perpetual hope. A season that sprang from an environment that was laden with oppression 2,000 years ago by the very same evil. Terrorism is certainly nothing new. Jesus was born into a world of violence and terrorism led by the Roman Empire. A murderous King Herod was ruler over the place where Jesus was born: Bethlehem. Oppression was the order of the day for the Jewish people. Violence was rudimentary to their way of life; it was feared and expected. But one day of violence came that no one could have ever imagined—the slaughter of the innocents.

A short time after Jesus was born, magi went into pursuit of Him in order to worship Him. They stopped in Jerusalem to ask King Herod if he knew where they might find this new baby king. Taken aback, Herod wore a façade of worshipful interest, saying he had no idea and asking the wise men to come back and tell him where they found the child so he, too, could worship him.

Well, the wise men were called wise for a reason. After finding the Christ child, they went home another way, bypassing Herod. Meanwhile, an angel told Joseph to take Mary and Jesus and flee to Egypt. Herod was furious when he found out about the wise men's departure. The evil and insanity within him welled up, and he ordered all male babies under the age of two in and around Bethlehem to be killed. If he couldn't find this baby king, he'd just kill them all to make sure a sword found him instead.

> Then what was said through the prophet Jeremiah was fulfilled: "A voice is heard in Ramah, weeping and great mourning, Rachel weeping for her children and *refusing to be comforted*, because they are no more." (Matthew 2:17–18, NIV, emphasis mine)

Imagine that. Imagine a bright sunny morning in Bethlehem. Imagine a mother sitting on the floor with her toddler, playing, laughing, and enjoying the love and delight of her life, rolled up in the smiling eyes of her little one. In an instant, the door crashes open, and a tall Roman soldier rushes in. He takes his bloodstained sword and slays the toddler before the mother's eyes. Then the soldier turns and leaves, slamming the door behind him. A scene, which moments ago had been one of happiness, suddenly turns to one of death and despair. All in an evil instant. The mother refused to be comforted because her child was no more.

A mother in 1941 gets the word that her son was killed in an instant in Pearl Harbor and is no more. A mother in 2001 gets the call that her daughter was on the 101st floor of the World Trade tower and is no more. Refusing to be comforted. Mothers felt it. Fathers felt it. Children felt it. Sisters, brothers, aunts, uncles, cousins, grandparents, friends felt it. Nations felt it. And I felt it. Days of infamy, all of them.

The War Within

So, after the initial feelings of overwhelming grief, what comes next? Anger. It is the natural progression of emotions. It is the natural response to make right, that which is wrong. To stop that which causes the hurt and the pain, so it doesn't happen again. Nations respond with war to defend their country and to pursue justice and are justified in stopping evil. Individuals respond with war as well, but it is a war within.

It's the individual war within that can become harder to justify. Oh, certainly we become motivated to take good, appropriate action. We raise money, we donate blood, and we mobilize causes to support our country and our citizens. We wear our patriotism on our sleeve and proudly display our flags on houses, cars, and buildings. We pray for our country and help those in need. When we do these things, it unites us as a people. It helps us to be comforted so we won't refuse to be comforted any longer. It is a beautiful thing to watch a nation rally together in one voice, one heart, headed toward one goal: victory. Perhaps this is a picture of what "be angry and not sin" looks like. Respond in the right way, in the justified way, to defeat evil. This is the good side of anger.

But there is the other side of anger that brings defeat in the war within. The anger, which motivated my patriotism, crossed the line. It led me to feelings I have never experienced. It led me to desire more than justice. It led me to desire vengeance, and as I've said before, that's God's business, not mine. It led me to hatred and a blind eye to seeing the innocents caught up in the snare of evil ones who were the true perpetrators. It led me to racism. And it led me far away from my God. Here I was, needing God the most in the days after the attack, yet I was unable to feel Him close to my heart because of the anger and hatred churning inside. Anger causes self-inflicted wounds when it goes too far. And the only way to be healed of those wounds is to let go of the anger. Just as a pendulum swings from one extreme to the other, the anger pendulum has to stop in the middle in order to regain balance.

As I was being tossed about on angry seas, I cried out to God, "Help me! Help me get hold of this anger! I need You back. I need emotional balance back. I need perspective back. For if I don't get these things back, my anger will be for naught, and I will be useless to myself and my country." God replied, "Do you think you're the only one who is struggling with this? You're not. And you're not only going to get over this, but you're also going to write about it. I never waste an experience with you. You will get your peace; you will get your balance at the proper time. But you must be willing to let your anger go and give it all to Me." But I liked the way my anger made me feel justified. I liked the way it gave me a reason to hate. But I didn't like how miserable it made me in the process.

Overboard

There is a familiar story you already know. It is a story about God's unconditional love and desire to bestow grace on all people, not just one favored nation. But this story has taken on a new meaning for me because I've come to realize that it is also a story about anger and running from God . . . and about me.

> The word of the LORD came to Jonah son of Amittai: "Go to the great city of Nineveh and preach against it, because its wickedness has come up before me." But Jonah ran away from the LORD and headed for Tarshish. He went down to Joppa, where he found a ship bound for that port. After paying the fare, he went aboard and sailed for Tarshish to flee from the LORD. (Jonah 1:1–3, NIV)

Let me stop here and give you some background. Jonah was an Israelite, one of God's chosen people. The Ninevites were hated enemies of the Israelites. They were among the cruelest in a long line of nations that terrorized Israel. God had had it with the Ninevites and couldn't stand their wickedness any longer. But He also loved them. They were still His creation, His children. So, He gave them one final chance to turn to the one true God. And that chance was bound up in an unwilling messenger named Jonah. But Jonah looked at the situation as a "fat chance," not a last chance. He was not about to allow his most hated enemy to be forgiven and loved by *his* God. And there was no way *he* was going to deliver the message. "I'll just run away. Yeah, that's the ticket! God will never find me. I'll dodge this assignment and my enemies will all die. What a *great* plan!"

So, Jonah hopped on a boat in Joppa. I've stood at that port in Joppa where Jonah got on board that boat. I've gazed out into those seas that turned angry. And I, like Jonah, have thought the very same, stupid thoughts. "Yeah, I'll hold on to my anger and hatred for my enemies and hide from God. I'll dodge this assignment to see my enemies as God sees them and to acknowledge the fact that He loves them as much as He loves me. Fat chance."

> Then the Lord sent a great wind on the sea, and such a violent storm arose that the ship threatened to break up. All the sailors were afraid, and each cried out to his own god. And they threw the cargo into the sea to lighten the ship. (Jonah 1:4–5, NIV)

Jonah runs and God pursues. God's anger at Jonah stirs the seas to get his attention. The pagan sailors (gasp, *pagan* sailors?!) panic and try to figure out what's going on. They draw lots to see who is responsible, and it falls to Jonah. They ask him, "What is the deal? Who *are* you? What have you done?!" Jonah had already told them that he was running from God. When he told them that he worshipped the Maker of all creation, including the seas, the sailors were afraid. Isn't it interesting? These nonbelievers were so eager and willing to accept God as the one, true God.

> The sea was getting rougher and rougher. So they asked him, "What should we do to you to make the sea calm down for us?" "Pick me up and throw me in the sea," he replied, "and it will become calm. I know that it is my fault that this great storm has come upon you." (Jonah 1:11–12, NIV)

And they did. The seas calmed, the sailors vowed to follow God, and God provided *Jonah* with a final chance—three days of thinking time in the belly of a large fish.

Jonah asked for God's forgiveness and said he would do as God told him to do from now on. So, when Jonah was back on dry land, God told him again to go to Nineveh. Jonah went and gave the word of warning to the people there. Jonah's worst fear came true. They responded. They turned to God and worshipped Him. God spared them and forgave them.

> But to Jonah this seemed very wrong, and he became angry. He prayed to the LORD, "Isn't this what I said, LORD, when I was still at home? That is what I tried to forestall by fleeing to Tarshish. I knew that you are a gracious and compassionate God, slow to anger and abounding in love, a God who relents from sending calamity. Now, LORD, take away my life, for it is better for me to die than to live." But the LORD replied, "Is it right for you to be angry?" (Jonah 4:1–4, NIV)

So, Jonah went out and pouted on a hillside, waiting to see what would happen. God provided a vine to quickly grow over Jonah and give him shade. The next day God made it a hot, sunny, scorcher. Jonah was miserable as his shady vine died. He told God he was miserable and would rather die than live without his vine! (Jonah definitely had some issues to work out.)

> But God said to Jonah, "Is it right for you to be angry about the plant?" "It is," he said. "And I'm so angry I wish I were dead." But the LORD said, "You have been concerned about this plant, though you did not tend it or make it grow. It sprang up overnight and died overnight. And should I not have concern for the great city of Nineveh, in which there are more than a hundred and twenty thousand people who cannot tell their right hand from their left—and also many animals?" (Jonah 4:9–11, NIV)

There the story ends. It ends with a question Jonah had to answer . . . that I had to answer.

What God wanted to happen from the very beginning happened: the enemy turned good. Jonah became angry and wanted to die. So, God put things into perspective: "What right do you have to be angry that these people turned to Me and were saved? You care more about a kudzu vine than you do about My children that I love as much as I love you."

Ouch. A few things to learn here. Jonah had an enemy that had hurt him. He had a right to be angry. But he did not have the right to be angry when they turned to God and were saved. Jonah wanted death for his enemy, not life. He wanted God's love all for himself and his people—not for the bad guys. God had to show him a different way to think and feel. And consider this. God's plan stopped terrorism because He changed the terrorist Ninevites from the inside out. *That* was the sore spot for Jonah. God took away his justification for anger. He couldn't hold onto it any longer.

As I relate Jonah's story to my own angry sea experience, I see the same sore spot. My anger is justified for what the terrorists did on 9/11. We as a nation are justified in going after them to defend our nation and to put a stop to terrorism. *That* is being angry and not sinning. Where I then internalized that anger to fierce hatred and a desire for the demise of all those people is where I let my anger turn to sin. I could not deal with the fact that God loved the hijackers that flew into the World Trade Center towers and the Pentagon as much as He loves me. How is that possible?! I had to come back to the reality of the nature of God.

He loves us because of who we are, not because of what we do, or don't do. He loves us because He made us, because we are His children. His anger will be stirred against us when we sin and turn from Him. He is a just God and will allow consequences to touch us that result from our sin. But as long as there is breath in the body of one of His own, He desires one more chance to have that one turn and run into His arms for forgiveness; one more chance to spend eternity in Heaven with Him. Sometimes people let their final chance pass them by, and God lets them go. However, He never stops wanting all of His children to come back. God is God because He is consistent and loving and just. If we desire Him to love and pursue us that way, then we must accept the fact that He offers this same love to all of mankind. He doesn't pick and choose based on our sin. Christ died for all—for all have sinned . . . you, the terrorists, me, all. In our world we have measures of good and evil by which to render judgment. In God's world all fall short apart from Christ—no exceptions. He wants ALL to be saved, not just those who know Him now. But all those who don't know Him at all and pursue evil. And there it was: there was my Jonah. It was time to toss my Jonah overboard.

You will not believe when I let go of my anger. And you will not believe *where* I let it go—at Ground Zero, New York City. I stood there at Ground Zero on the 60th anniversary of Pearl Harbor, December 7, 2001. I looked at the ruins of the World Trade Center. I walked along the memorial wall and looked at pictures of the faces of those who were missing and were lost. I read the words of those in grief, of those refusing to be comforted. I wrote some words of my own: "God's heart was the first to break . . . " I saw a tee shirt that said, "God Loves NY." Oh, how He does! I peered into the eyes and souls of the NYPD and rescue workers there. I saw their grief and their exhaustion, but I saw something more. I saw their determination and resolve. I saw their hope that what had happened here in this hallowed place wouldn't be for naught. That those who were lost would be remembered, that justice would be achieved, and that the very spirit which made this city of New York and this country great would be restored and strengthened to a level perhaps not seen in a generation or more. These New Yorkers who had experienced their own slaughter of the innocents firsthand were keeping their anger in check. They were motivated to do what needed to be done to move forward. They were not immobilized and tossed about on angry seas. They were plowing through those rough waters full steam ahead.

As I walked from Ground Zero to Battery Park to get the ferry to New York Harbor, a strange thing happened. The prison doors on my spirit opened. I began to feel my hands get around the neck of my anger for the first time. A strange peace entered my soul. As the Miss New York ferryboat left the dock, I looked at the skyline of New York City and at the void where two tall towers once proudly stood. My gaze drifted to Ellis Island, and my mind swarmed with millions of people from all nations who came to this country through that portal—millions who left oppression and angry seas behind to start a new life here. And then, she appeared. Lady Liberty. That Statue which stands strong and proud, symbolizing the strength and goodness of this land that I love. Never had she been more beautiful, more precious to me.

It was time. In the middle of New York Harbor, I tossed my Jonah of anger overboard. My angry seas were calmed, and a dam burst in my spirit. My perspective returned to me. My emotional balance returned to me. And God's presence was strongly entrenched in my heart. It was at Christmas time in New York that God brought peace into my pain and calmed my angry seas. Coming face to face with where it all happened but more importantly to whom it all happened allowed me to be comforted in a strange way. As I rode in that yellow taxicab to catch my plane home, I gazed at flags hung from Park Avenue to the projects along the highway. It warmed my heart. I saw one nation, under God, indivisible, with liberty and justice for all.

As Christmas neared, I thought a lot about these things: the days of infamy, anger, and people's responses across time. No, I'm not the only one who has been tossed on angry seas. Jesus was born into a storm filled with them. Jonah was tossed on the angry seas of his own making. You may be dealing with anger that stems from a totally different source than mine. Yours might be much older in nature, too. You might have been holding onto your anger since childhood. Hurts you couldn't let go. People and experiences you couldn't get beyond. Step back and look at your life. You were hurt, you reacted. But now the source of hurt may be long gone from your life. Still, you hang on tightly to your anger. And what has it brought you? Perpetual hurt from a time long ago. You've not only been robbed once; you've allowed yourself to be robbed numerous times since from self-inflicted wounds that harm no one but you. Isn't it time to let it go?

Whatever caused your anger, respond to it appropriately now if you didn't do so then. Do what is justified in response. Be moved to a proper course of action to set it right. But then, let it go. Don't hold on to it any longer. It's time to calm those angry seas. Once hurricanes have served their balancing purpose, they blow out and extinguish themselves. If they blew beyond their good and proper purpose, their continued angry seas would negate any good that would have come from their existence.

Jesus came into our world to bring peace into our pain, to fill our hungry souls, to heal us, and to save us. I hope you will welcome Him into your world. Toss your anger overboard, and your angry seas will be calmed by the perfect Son of God.

I must go down to the seas again, to the lonely sea and the sky
And all I ask is a tall ship and a star to steer her by;
And the wheel's kick and the wind's song and the white sails shaking,
And a gray mist on the sea's face, and a gray dawn breaking.
I must go down to the seas again, for the call of the running tide
Is a wild call and a clear call that may not be denied;
And all I ask is a windy day with the white clouds flying,
And the flung spray and the blown spume, and the sea-gulls crying.
I must go down to the seas again, to the vagrant gypsy life,
To the gull's way and the whale's way where the wind's
like a whetted knife;
And all I ask is a merry yarn from a laughing fellow-rover,
And quiet sleep and a sweet dream when the long trick's over.

—John Masefield, Sea-Fever[1]

Chapter 13

SEASICK

Sea Fever

Sea fever. The writer of this poem had a bad case of this sentimental ailment. And if you haven't noticed, the writer of this book has it, too. I love the sea and everything about it. It would be hard for me to think of anything that would make me love it any more or any less. Like Masefield, I can't resist the call of the sea and must go down to the seas again and again.

Being near the sea has given me joy, but it has also given me pain. The sting of a jellyfish, the misery of a bad sunburn, the irritation of mosquito bites, and a dreadful case of sea fever. I mean *literal* sea fever. Last summer I joined my parents on the South Carolina coast for some time on our sailboat, *Agape*. While there I enjoyed some time at the beach, but unfortunately, I didn't realize that I was swimming in bad ocean water. Pollution has long touched our rivers, streams, and lakes; now it has reached our seas. While I was gleefully body surfing in the waves, some wicked bacteria were gleefully body surfing in me. By dinner I had a sore throat; by bedtime I had a headache, and by midnight I had a raging fever.

A debilitating sinus infection landed me in bed for two weeks. My doctor tried an antibiotic and the bacteria smirked. He tried a stronger drug, and the bacteria defiantly stood its ground. My doctor then brought out the big guns: the last resort, strongest medicine on the market, and finally the bacteria gave in. It couldn't resist the power of this medicine, so it left my body. I finally had quiet sleep and sweet dreams because the long trick was over.

The sea made me sick. The very place I love and hold so dear to my heart turned on me and slapped me down. I have never encountered anything like that before. Do you think this experience made me resent the sea and love it any less? Of course not. In fact, this experience did the very opposite. It grieved me to learn that this part of the sea is sick and needs help. It didn't turn me away . . . it drew me closer. It made me want to find out what needs to be done to heal the sea and restore it back to health.

The Great Physician

Today is Good Friday, 3:00 p.m. to be exact. This is the day that Jesus was turned on, slapped down, and nailed to a tree by those He loved so very much and held so dear to His heart. He had wanted nothing more than to gleefully revel in the sheer presence of those He created and loved more than life itself. He taught them, nurtured them, healed their wounds, and showed them grace and unconditional love. But these people—you and I included as part of humankind—were sick. We were sick with the fever of sin, and there was no cure. Our fevered minds and hearts were so distorted with this illness that we couldn't think straight . . . or feel straight. Jesus knew this. He even said so. While hanging on the cross, looking through blood-filled eyes, He looked up toward Heaven and said, "Father, forgive them, for they do not know what they are doing" (Luke 23:34, NIV). He knew how sick we were, and He knew that He was the only one who could cure us. He was the big gun antibiotic who could once and for all put an end to the plague of sin and death. No, we didn't know what we were doing when we killed the Great Physician—the only One who could help us. That would be insane, now, wouldn't it? We didn't know what we were doing because it wasn't our plan in the first place. It was God's.

An Apple a Day

With the first bite of forbidden fruit, perhaps an apple, in the Garden of Eden, God pulled out the prescription pad and began writing. With the very first sin of Eve, God knew what had to be done. Before that bite of apple had slidden down her throat and settled in her stomach, the plan was done. For God knew an apple a day would keep The Doctor away . . . and that was unacceptable.

No, we didn't know what we were doing when Jesus was arrested, and we all ran away and denied we knew Him, like Peter, or when we ripped Jesus' back to shreds with a whip, or when we pushed a cap of one-inch thorns deep into His scalp, blinding Him with His own blood. No, we didn't know what we were doing when we mocked Him, spit on Him, kicked Him, and beat Him. Or when we drove spikes through His wrists and feet. Or when we removed His dignity along with His clothes. We didn't know what we were doing when we allowed Him to hang there for six hours while we looked on and mocked Him. We didn't know what we were doing while His arms were overstretched, and His ribcage was expanded beyond comfort so He couldn't breathe. We didn't know what we were doing as His lungs filled with fluid, and He drowned there on the cross in agony. We didn't know what was really taking place, that He was not only drowning in His lungs—He was drowning in our sin. He was drowning in a sea of despair because at one moment He was slapped with the knowledge of every sin you and I have ever committed, will commit in the next five minutes, and will commit until we die.

We didn't know that His Father who had never left His side did so at the most agonizing moment of His life. We didn't know that the God of Heaven wept bitterly when He had to turn His back on His only Son because holiness and sin are incompatible. And we really didn't know that while Jesus was enduring all of this, His love for you and me was never stronger. He felt no resentment or love lost for us over what we had done. He felt love and hope for us because of what *He* had done.

The prescription that was written long ago in the Garden was filled and dispensed that Friday, a day called "Good" because a cure was found for the incurable. No longer would we have to be eternally sick without the medicine to make us well. We didn't know what we were doing then, but we should know now. Or do we?

Do we know what we're doing when we turn our backs on Him if we deny that we are His followers when it becomes uncomfortable? It may not be an outright verbal denial like Peter's. It may be our silence when we have an opportunity to speak up. Do we realize that we mock Him if we use His name in vain as we curse the afternoon traffic? Do we know that we hurt Him when we refuse to do as He directs, preferring to have things our way? Do we understand that it breaks His heart when we neglect those in need when it is in our power to help? If we don't know by now, we'd better go back to the beginning and read from the Garden to the Cross. Our sins are paid for, but as we commit each one, we should wince . . . Jesus did. That should be enough for us to know . . . and for us to think twice before we make a move.

No one can take our medicine for us. We must choose to take it ourselves. Oh, we can try other medicines, like good works, to try to cure our sick souls, but ultimately their placebo effect won't save us. Only the big gun antibiotic of grace from the Great Physician can do that. This medicine is easy to take and has an immediate effect. When you take this precious medicine into your sick soul, you will finally have a quiet sleep and sweet dreams because the long trick will be over.

Get well soon.

He led me beside salt water; He restored my soul.

—Jenny L. Cote, March 11, 2000, Hilton Head, S.C.

Chapter 14

SALVAGE AFTER THE STORM

Have you ever had one of those days? Or months? Or years? Those times when you are slammed with bad news, difficult situations, or impossible realities? Of course you have. I have, we all have. Those times or storms are woven into the fabric of every life. What makes the storms unique is how the individual reacts to them.

We all react better to situations we can get our hands around. We are better able to cope with situations that we can define. I think the reason is that once you have a problem defined, you can better find a solution to address it. Wouldn't it be great if we could do that with life storms? I think we can.

Allow me to borrow a defining tool from the meteorological world. The Saffir-Simpson Damage-Potential Scale was developed in the early 1970's by a consulting engineer (Herbert Saffir) and the then Director of the National Hurricane Center (Dr. Robert Simpson). It defines hurricanes based on wind speeds and it estimates barometric pressure and storm surge associated with five categories.[1] These categories are 1) minimal, 2) moderate, 3) extensive, 4) extreme, and 5) catastrophic. Each category gives descriptions of damage potential and recommended courses of action. This scale has been tremendously useful in helping people to understand the strength and power of approaching storms and how to act accordingly.

Why not do the same with life storms? Try it sometime. Figure out if a storm headed your way is simply a tropical depression that won't even make the damage scale, a moderate Category 2, or a catastrophic Category 5. Perhaps it will give you a handle on what you are facing and what measures you need to take to see it through.

Storms will vary from person to person and from situation to situation. I would not begin to presume to tell you how to specifically weather them. There are three certainties that I can give you, however. One certainty is that God doesn't make inferior vessels. The material from which He made your hull can withstand whatever storms head your way. He made some hulls stronger than others; the stronger ones can handle stronger storms. He will *never* allow more than you can handle while He is at the helm, OK? Gain peace from that fact. But, to ensure the integrity of the hull in a storm, He does require vessel oversight. So, keep Him at the helm.

The second certainty is that He hears you and knows every aspect of your storm. Chuck Swindoll once said, "A teardrop from earth summons the king of heaven." Let that soak in. He knows. And He stops whatever He is doing with the cosmos at the time to hear you. Just as a loving parent runs to the side of a hurt child, so too, does your heavenly Father run to you.

The other certainty is that no storm will last forever. But, while it is raging, you must weather the storm, one way or another. Some people might think they can avoid a storm by ignoring it, but that is rather foolhardy, don't you think? Can you envision a sailor during a Category 4 hurricane saying, "What, this? This isn't a storm! It's a spring shower. I don't need to do anything." Seems to me he'd quickly become acquainted with the ocean floor.

When storms come, you need to be prepared. Have your rigging secure and keep a close eye on your vessel for any weak spots that need immediate attention. Batten down the hatches, hold on, and steer the best you can. And most importantly, pray. God will most certainly guide you through to a safe haven.

After the storm comes the calm and usually, a mess. It always amazes me to watch film footage of areas slammed by hurricanes after the storm has moved on. Houses are swept away from their foundations; beaches are eroded; once-strong trees are now projectile arrows into buildings, and there is water, water, everywhere. My parents moved to Myrtle Beach, South Carolina, shortly after Category 4 Hurricane Hugo dealt a devastating blow to the Grand Strand. Over the course of many visits there, I slowly saw the beach heal with new palm trees and new sand dunes formed with the help of swaying sea oats, and sand-hugging morning glories.

Sand was dredged and pumped in from a mile offshore to replenish the beach. At first the sand was an icky gray color but became sun-bleached white after a time. It was rather fun to pick up unusual fossils and sharks' teeth by the handful from the imported deep-sea sand.

The storm came. It left a mess. Cleanup was required. And the beach healed. Care to translate this stormy lesson to our lives? The parallel is the same. We've already said that storms will come, so expect them, and ride them out the best you can. Now, what about the mess?

The mess will depend on not only the strength of the storm, but also how well you handled it. Sometimes the cleanup will be quick, sometimes lengthy. But let me challenge you to welcome the cleanup. In fact, look forward to it! Celebrate that the storm is over, and you survived. Just as it was fun finding treasured shark teeth in the beach cleanup, find treasures for your spirit as you dredge fresh sand back onto your beach. Salvaging not only restores; it makes your beach better than it was before.

The new millennium was an exciting time, wasn't it? The expectations of a New Year, a new century, and a new millennium were sometimes fearful, but mostly exciting. Let me share a Category 2 life storm that crept into my millennium when it was barely three hours old. At 3:00 a.m. on January 1, 2000, I became violently ill, I think from food poisoning. I had a rough six hours that was worse than any seasickness could ever be. Just as relief came at 10:00 a.m. I got a phone call that my dear "2nd father," Jack, had died in the night. We had been expecting Jack's death, so it was not a surprise. That didn't make it any easier. He was my dad's best friend, and he and Dot were as close to a second set of parents as you could get. Jack made me laugh, made me mad, taught me about music, and always answered my crazy whims. He would take me riding on the back of his motorcycle on back roads, going 70 miles per hour. I would say, "Faster, faster!" And he always obliged. (Sorry, mom!) So, my new millennium was not exactly off to a stellar beginning.

Going through that loss was difficult. Next came some difficult work pressures that kicked up the wind and the waves even higher. Then two more funerals. Meanwhile, some of my dearest friends experienced storms of their own that I happily helped them weather, but it left me drained. Then on February 2nd I had to have my thirteen-year-old cat put to sleep. Cally developed cancer and went down rather quickly. My grief in unexpectedly saying goodbye to this dear friend was so hard, especially on top of an already bruised heart. I didn't feel much like celebrating my birthday a couple of days later. I looked and sounded very much like Eeyore the donkey with his gloomy outlook.

My vessel began to develop leaks. My perspective became out of sorts. Issues that were no big deal under normal circumstances seemed larger than life. I think I even felt my mast crack. I could see exactly what was happening. The storm of several issues piled on top of one another began to take its toll. But finally, finally, I saw calmer waters ahead. I thought, "Just hold on a little longer." And I did. But I was a mess.

You see, God is way ahead of us. He knows how much we can take, and He goes before us to prepare salvage set-up long before the storm is over. God knew that by March, I would need to regroup. Months earlier, I had planned a weekend getaway by myself in Hilton Head, S.C., following business in Savannah at the end of April. Due to a schedule change, I moved up my business trip from late April to early March. Or rather, *He* moved it. Not only had I been through the storm, but it had also been ten months since I had been to the coast; my soul was aching beyond belief by then. God always, without fail, provides me passage back to the coast just when I need it.

So, on Friday morning, March 10th, I checked into an oceanfront resort in Hilton Head, South Carolina, threw on my bathing suit, grabbed my beach chair and my new book and headed down to the beach. I got my toes in the sand, took a deep breath of salt air, opened my book, closed my book, and fell asleep in the sun.

When I woke up, the first thing I did was cry. I cried tears of grief from the storm. I cried tears of joy that it was over. I cried tears of relief and gratefulness to be alone with my heavenly Father at the beach. He sat there in the beach chair with me and just held me. We talked for a long time. I told Him all I had been through. He listened and kissed my cheek with gentle breezes now and then to empathize with me. Then we talked about the salvage, and what I needed to do. And you know what He said?

"Do nothing. Rest, pray, and refill your well. It is only your emotions that are a mess, nothing else." I had no relational messes to clean up, no situational problems to deal with. I just had a heart covered in seaweed to clean off. The relief came pouring out of my spirit like a mighty dredge, bringing fresh sand back to my beach. I did as God told me to. Over the course of the next day, I took a long walk, observed nature, found a perfect sand dollar, slept, took a long swim, read my book, got in the hot tub, showered, ordered room service, watched a movie, and had a long night's sleep. I did nothing but focus on vessel repair.

Guess what God then did for me? He sent another storm, but this time one I did not have to endure. He sent a literal storm that blocked my driving path to get home. I had originally planned to spend one night and go home Saturday afternoon. As I was preparing to check out, I turned on the weather report to see a perfectly outlined rectangle of potentially tornadic storms across my entire route home. I had to stay another night in Hilton Head rather than risk the drive. God had determined that the salvage was incomplete.

So, I did more of the same vessel repair the second day. I took my 7:00 a.m. power walk. I went past some seagulls feeding on some decaying fish heads that had washed ashore. One squawked at me as I walked by, and I said, "Don't worry, pal, *I* don't want any!" That was *their* cleanup duty, not mine. Throughout the rest of the day, I read, prayed, and swam. When evening came, God wanted me to go visit a love of mine. I went to Harbor Town for dinner and heard some great music: "Changes in Latitudes," among others. Then I went walking around the marina to visit my love: rows of beautiful sailboats.

The music I heard outside was even better than what I heard inside. The wind was softly blowing; water was gently lapping against strong hulls, and boat lines were creaking. Not a soul was around. I went and sat down on a storage box next to a 40-foot sloop named *Abracadabra.* I just sat there and listened. I listened to the wind and to the ropes creaking. I held on to the spring line and empathized with that beautiful boat that wanted to be free of restricting dock lines. Then I began to sob and sob and sob. With every tear, I felt release. And then it dawned on me—I was empathizing because I was ready to go out on the open sea once again. My vessel was repaired and longing to get back out where it was meant to be, sailing with full sails and ready for any storm, come what may. Just as salt water heals physical wounds, it also healed my emotional ones simply with its presence.

On the third day, my salvage was complete, it was time to go home. But not before God gave me one last gift. It was a brisk, windy morning. The wind snatched words away from passerby as soon as they were uttered. But sitting there, writing in my journal, I heard an unusual sound coming down the beach. It was the sound of bagpipes. And those bagpipes were playing "Amazing Grace." My seaweed-free heart smiled, and I hummed right along. I had my Sunday morning worship right there, in my favorite place in the entire world, the beach. I had to know where this bagpipe player was from, so I went and asked him. He was from the Chesapeake, my "sea hometown." It was a loving reminder that I can always go home to the sea when I need it and receive amazing grace. What an incredible ending to my salvage experience!

I came across a scripture that really spoke to me. Not only is God way ahead of us, but He's also way behind us, too. Meaning, He's been there, done that. Listen to this: "When Jesus heard what had happened, he withdrew by boat privately to a solitary place" (Matthew 14:13, NIV). He had just lost His friend, John the Baptist. His heart was grieving, and He had to regroup after the storm of such a loss. He went to the sea alone. And I'm sure His Father held Him just as He held me. He listened to Jesus and told Him to do nothing but rest, pray, and refill His well. I'm sure that the same soft breezes kissed Jesus' cheek as God soothed His hurting heart.

Jesus Himself knew the importance of salvage after the storm. The very Creator of the storms had to stop and regroup from the aftermath. After He had done so, and landed on the other side of the sea, His vessel was repaired and strong enough to feed 5,000 people with five loaves of bread and two fish.

Listen to what happened next. After His impromptu dinner party of 5,000, Jesus sent His disciples ahead of Him by boat while He went away again to a mountaintop to pray and regroup.

> After he had dismissed them, he went up on a mountainside by himself to pray. Later that night, he was there alone, and the boat

> was already a considerable distance from land, buffeted by the waves because the wind was against it. Shortly before dawn Jesus went out to them, walking on the lake. When the disciples saw him walking on the lake, they were terrified. "It's a ghost," they said, and cried out in fear. But Jesus immediately said to them: "Take courage! It is I. Don't be afraid." "Lord, if it's you," Peter replied, "tell me to come to you on the water." "Come," he said. Then Peter got down out of the boat, walked on the water and came toward Jesus. But when he saw the wind, he was afraid and, beginning to sink, cried out, "Lord, save me!" Immediately Jesus reached out his hand and caught him. "You of little faith," he said, "why did you doubt?" And when they climbed into the boat, the wind died down. (Matthew 14:23–32, NIV)

Jesus not only regrouped from one storm, but He also walked all over the next one. And then made it stop.

God not only helps us salvage our minds and hearts after storms; He makes us stronger than we were before. He sends us back out to do what we were made to do; not staying in port all the time restricted by dock lines, but sailing freely on open, shiny blue seas to revel in life. And fully prepared for the next storm.

So, be prepared for *your* next storm. It will come. Or, if you are in a storm right now, hang on. Define it. How bad is it, really? A tropical depression? A Category 3 storm? Whatever the strength, weather it with God at the helm. Then go away and salvage yourself from the emotional mess. Be sure to allow God to be your travel agent for the getaway package. After a time, your beach will heal, and your vessel will be ready to set sail.

Anchors aweigh, my friend. Anchors aweigh.

PART FOUR

GOING ASHORE

"A day at the beach is never lost time."

"All you need is a good dose of vitamin sea."

"Happy as a seagull with a French fry."

"If you're not barefoot, then you're overdressed."

"Beach hair, don't care."

"A day at the beach restores the soul."

—Unknown

The sea awoke at midnight from its sleep,
And round the pebbly beaches far and wide
I heard the first wave of the rising tide
Rush onward with uninterrupted sweep;
A voice out of the silence of the deep,
A sound mysteriously multiplied
As of a cataract from the mountain's side,
Or roar of winds upon a wooded steep.
So comes to us at times, from the unknown
And inaccessible solitudes of being,
The rushing of the sea-tides of the soul;
And inspirations, that we deem our own,
Are some divine foreshadowing and foreseeing
Of things beyond our reason or control.

—*The Sound of the Sea,* Henry Wadsworth Longfellow[1]

Chapter 15

SOUND OF THE SOUL

Yes siree, Henry. Now *there* was a man after my own heart. He speaks my language. I appreciate his wisdom. And I hear exactly what he hears.

Can you hear it? What do you mean *what*? Oh, wait—is there any noise where you are right now? Well, don't read another word until you are free from all man-made noise. You need to be where you can hear it. If you're outside and away from a lot of people, *especially* at the beach, you're fine. Otherwise, go ahead and close the book and get somewhere quiet. I'll be right here when you get back.

Hmmm . . .

Glad you're back. OK, now . . . do you hear it? Listen very hard. It's called a "quiet moment."

Rare, aren't they? Now, close your eyes for a moment . . . and just listen. Take in five slow, deep breaths and slowly let them go. Take as long as you want. I'll still be here.

What you are experiencing is vital for your soul. It is vital for your mind. It is vital for your body. It is the time of being still. It is the time of listening to nothing but the sounds of God's creation, echoed in the beating of your heart. It is the time for listening to that still, small voice. There is much that your soul is longing to hear, and when it is wrapped in your attentive silence, it finally has the chance to listen.

Most of us know at a very deep level that our souls and lives cry out for such stillness. Yet how often do you give yourself this vital experience? If you're like most people, the answer probably is "not very much." Why? Why do we always talk about how stressed out we are, how busy we are, how jam-packed our schedules are, and how we barely have any time to get our daily chores done, much less do anything personally for ourselves? It has gotten just as bad as the cliché about the weather: everyone talks about it, but no one does anything about it.

But unlike the weather, this is one area of my life in which I can make a difference. In fact, I have made a concerted effort to incorporate regular times of quiet listening into my often-hectic routine. I *have* to. I crave it too deeply not to. I am such a paradox—on the one hand I'm as outgoing as they come. Anyone who knows me will testify that I will chat with anything that moves. My verbosity is never lacking, it seems. But I also have a side that must be alone, that treasures solitude. As with all the rest of creation, I instinctively seek states of equilibrium. And in my semiconscious quest for equilibrium, I think I learned early in life to stop and listen.

When I go to the coast, listening is one of the things I enjoy most. Longfellow had it right in his poem. The sound of the sea becomes the sound of my soul. In the quiet solitude of my spirit there is an indescribable realization of mind and heart. The sounds of the sea are not all I hear; they simply, beautifully, create the ambience for listening to my spirit—and to my Maker and Guide.

Let me offer you some ambience right now. As you read, listen.

You're at the beach at dusk. Everyone has left for the day, and you've stayed behind for a while. You're alone. The sky today was as clear and blue as you've ever seen it. But now, soft pink clouds are making their way over to the sun to gently put it to bed for the night. You hear waves rolling into shore. They break with echoing crashes, and then fizz as they dissolve into the sand. The salt perfumes the gentle breeze that blows softly in your face. Sometimes you hear signs of the breeze around you, and sometimes you hear it breathing directly in your ears. You're sitting close enough to the water so you can hear the shells rolling and clinking together in the beach-landing waves. Up above you a pair of gulls call—having a great time—talking and laughing about what they might find for dinner. Right beside your beach chair, a ghost crab runs along the sand and darts into his cavernous hole because you've just spotted him. Out in the water you've been watching a pelican skim the surface of the sea, magically hovering an inch above it with unmatched grace, in perfect sync with every rising wave. He turns upward and soars into the sky. Suddenly, he dive-bombs toward the water, and lands with a mighty splash! He's found *his* dinner. The school of fish he dove into scatters in disarray, sputtering across the water's sunset-colored surface in a staccato rhythm. Out past the horizon you see a light appear in the twilight sky—it is the North Star. You feel something stir inside you—it's your soul—knocking and saying, "Is the coast clear? Can I come out now?" You tell it, "Oh yes, the *coast* is very clear. Come on out."

Got the ambience? Now, let's hear some more Longfellow wisdom:

> Sit in reverie and watch the changing color of the waves that break upon the idle seashore of the mind.[2]

I *love* this guy. Sit in reverie (joyful solitude). Watch the changing color of the waves (your soul) that break upon the idle seashore of the mind. When you are still, when you cannot just witness but absorb the majesty of God that permeates every creation, your mind can finally become idle. The changing color of your soul can break through. It is free to get some much-needed attention. Like Longfellow you will notice that you not only can hear the beautiful sound of the sea—you hear the beautiful sound of your soul.

The sound of my soul comes out in layers. The initial layers are ones of joy and exuberance, of thankfulness and delight. I simply sit in reverie of those emotions. As time passes, the layers become deeper. Longings of my soul are released for exploration. Dreams. Hopes. Desires. Sheer creativity. I feel as if I can do anything that I imagine.

Once these longings come out, God—the original North Star—appears on my horizon.

The North Star has guided sailors around the world since they first dared to believe there was something more beyond their familiar horizons. From season to season, the North Star never moves but always provides a fixed bearing that sailors can trust in their navigations. Just so, God begins to speak to my heart, leading me in the right direction.

Like countless spiritual travelers before me, I feel that I am not alone in my reverie. God sits in reverie with me. But while I enter this peaceful place through the ambience of the sea, God tells me He is there to partake of the wonders of another creation. His presence is focused on the ambience of *me*. Together we listen to my heart's needs. He answers each longing in turn, allowing me to see the possibilities. If it is a longing to accomplish something, He encourages me with insight as to how I could make it a reality. If it is a longing for healing from a wounded heart, He fills me with peace and comfort, and washes away my hurt just like a wave fizzes in the sand.

Sometimes this quiet time is light. Sometimes it is heavy. But it is always full of joy. It is never as intense for me as it is at the coast. That is why I must get back to the coast whenever I can—my soul *must* be heard, and it speaks most clearly by the sea. As I said in the prologue, any of God's landscapes can serve as a soul-connection. You can feel God most strongly wherever that landscape is in your ideal world. Wherever that is, go there and listen. Let your soul come out for a while. Let it speak.

But, if you're like me, there's a lot of time in between those visits to your special place. What do you do to capture that vital quietness for your spirit? Well, you make time for quietness by making it a priority. I encourage you to do it daily. I get up at 6:00 a.m. each day before my guys rise and shine. I make some flavored coffee and go sit in my beach room. Yes, I said, "beach room." I chose a place in my house to be my haven. My regular quiet time is so important to me; why would I not create a special, encouraging place for it?

Everything in the room is related to the sea—framed coastal prints, family pictures of happy times at the beach, baskets and sand buckets filled to the brim with seashells, sailboats, lighthouses, nautical signs, shell lamps, my salty old sailor figurine, etc. It's like a "mini-beach." I play soft music set to ocean sound—surf, gulls, and dolphins. I envisioned this room years ago . . . while sitting on the beach. So, for my in-between time, I have a small room that mirrors the ambience of the real thing. Maybe I went a little *overboard,* but hey, it *floats my boat!*

Find a place in your home where you can comfortably sit and where your mind will be most likely to idle. And if you wish, put something nearby that helps carry you toward that which your soul holds dear. It might be a single framed picture. It might be music. Just something to serve as a soul-reminder.

The coastal setting is there for my daily quiet time, self-manufactured as it is. But two genuine spirits are also there—God's and mine—and that part is the same as when I'm at the beach. I write in my journal, and I read God's word. I pray, and I listen. And God speaks just as dearly. He gives me what I need for the day ahead. God always leads me to Scriptures that miraculously address a specific concern or give me encouragement I will need in the coming 24 hours. Yes, the time is briefer than my coastal experiences, and perhaps the soul layers don't go as deep, but the daily joy is still there.

If you aren't having this encounter with God every day, your soul will erode without you even realizing it. You'll wonder what is wrong with you—why you are so stressed, strung out, and unable to focus. Our bodies need food and water every day to grow and thrive. If your body were malnourished, you would fix that, wouldn't you? You would give your body what it needs. Well, it's not much different for the soul, except that the required nourishment is quiet time with God. If I start my day without quiet time, nothing feels right all day. But giving my soul what it needs at the outset of the day never fails to create in me mental clarity, emotional energy, and stability. Only then do I feel fully equipped for my day. When you have that kind of beginning, it doesn't matter what comes your way: you're ready.

You may protest, "Well, that sounds great, but I just don't have the time." No, you choose whether to have the time or not. I long ago memorized Proverbs 10:27: "Reverence the Lord and He will add hours to your day." Somehow, when you give Him the first fruits of your time, He multiplies it throughout the day. Your efficiency is enhanced. Your ability to focus and accomplish things is multiplied. He honors your decision to give Him the time of your day.

If your soul is malnourished, feed it. You should be able to hear it loud and clear. Your place and time might be different than mine, but the importance for your soul is the same. Don't wait for occasional trips to feed your soul, either. That would be like binge eating! Give it what it needs daily. And remember—our souls are eternal, not our bodies.

I'm going to be quiet now so maybe you'll have some time to practice what I preach. I began with some poetry about the sounds of the sea. I'd like to leave you with some words for the sound of the soul:

> "Be still and know that I am God" (Psalm 46:10, NIV).

> May your joy be as deep as the ocean, and your sorrow as light as its foam. —*Unknown*

For I am the LORD*, your God,*
who takes hold of your right hand and says to you,
Do not fear; I will help you.

—Isaiah 41:13, NIV

Chapter 16

A WALK ALONG THE BEACH

Imagine That

Have you ever paused to consider how blessed we are to have an imagination? As children our imagination made playtime an endless adventure. We could be explorers in the Amazon before jumping into our spaceship to save the Earth from invading aliens with our laser-infused shields. We'd race back to Earth in time for our date with Ken and Barbie while stopping along the way to spend $1 million on a new car and groovy clothes. Of course, after dinner we'd join Jacques Cousteau on a deep-sea salvage expedition in the bathtub, recovering untold treasures while evil pirates waited for us back up at the surface. Sometimes there were scary monsters in the closet or under the bed, but daylight usually made them go away.

Ah, how rich is that? What a gift—imagination! I'm sitting in my beach room, watching Alex have a major battle with his Rockem' Sockem' Robots. He's oblivious to me. Of course, that's because he's in another galaxy at the moment. The G.I. Joes have all been briefed and prepared for the invasion of these alien robots. Enjoy it, Alex. Revel in your childhood imagination for as long as possible.

What's great about imagination is that even when we leave childhood, our imagination comes with us. It just grows up to match our adult perspective. Oh, we can still become explorers in the Amazon, jump into spaceships, have dream dates and shopping sprees, deep sea adventures and fight bad guys. And be afraid. But all these things become idea launching pads that we can pursue into reality. A dream is born when it is imagined.

"What if I could . . . ?" You fill in the blank. It's great with the fun stuff, isn't it? We envision what we'd like to be, where we'd like to go, how we'd get there, and what we'd do when we arrive. But what about the scary stuff?

"What if I could . . . overcome my fear of failure with this new job? New boss? New class? New spouse? New move? New loneliness? You fill in the blank. When you finish filling in the blank, guess who's standing there waiting on the other side of the question mark? God. He's there after the question marks of the fun stuff, too. But sometimes we most need to be reminded of His presence after the scary, hard questions.

I have such a desire to see God. I can't wait to bust through the gates of Heaven, saying, "Dad, I'm home!" then run straight into the arms of Jesus, wrapping my arms around His neck, squeezing Him tightly, hearing Him chuckle and say, "Hi, glad you made it—welcome home!" Then I want to look deeply into His eyes and tell Him how much I love Him. Then, of course, I'll proceed to talk His ear off with the multitude of questions I have.

I know that will happen someday, but I have a desire to see God here and now. My imagination helps me do that. Sometimes when I'm really hurting or just really aching to feel close to God, perhaps when I've strayed away from Him, guess where I meet Him? For a long walk along the beach. I close my eyes and am transported instantly to the coast. I walk over the sand dune; that gentle sea breeze hits my face, and He's there waiting for me. He's standing at the water's edge gazing out into the sea. But then He sees me, smiles, waves, and walks toward me. When He reaches me, He cups my face in both hands and looks deeply into my eyes. He says, "Look right here—focus on Me. Let's go for a walk." He drops His hands and reaches down to take mine. And together we just walk along the beach.

I've come to realize that when I do this, I'm just animating my prayers. I just talk to Jesus and tell Him everything that's on my heart. This is especially comforting when I'm afraid. How do I know that this imagination-fueled scenario—personal, even intimate—is in keeping with God's wishes? I have many reasons. One of my favorites is this verse:

> "For I am the LORD, *your* God, who takes hold of *your* right hand and says to *you*, Do not fear; I will help *you*" (Isaiah 41:13, NIV, emphasis mine).

Did you notice all the times God mentions *you*? Wow—let's look at what He's really saying . . .

I'm All Yours

"I am the LORD, your God . . ." He shoots straight about exactly who He is. He wants you to gain comfort in knowing who He is, and what He is. He's not some linguini-spined, sometimes dependable lord. No—He's 100 percent powerful and reliable. He is Lord—sovereign, omniscient, creator, protector, director, and lover of your soul. You can therefore trust what He is about to say.

He is *your* God. Now why would He say that? "Your" implies ownership or possession. This relationship is personal! He's not a distant being off in another galaxy and untouchable and unreachable by you. He's *yours*.

I submit that, often, what some people imagine about God isn't close to reality. If you've imagined God as a stern old man with a long white beard, sitting on a throne with a scowl on His face and a bucket of lightning bolts—just waiting for you to mess up so He could nail you—you have Him all wrong. Look at this next snapshot of what He *really* is like.

I Wanna Hold Your Hand

". . . Who takes hold of your right hand . . ." God is the one who acts here. He wants to hold your hand. The Creator of all things wants a personal connection with you! He doesn't take anyone else's hand on your behalf—He takes yours into His. Now, when you take someone by the hand—not a handshake, but an intimate clasp—how do you feel? Do you do this with someone you dislike or are indifferent to? No! You do this with someone you care for, someone you love, or someone you are deeply concerned about. Just imagine how God must feel about you to say such a thing! Billions of people have lived across time, and God in His *greatness* knows every one of them. Yet in His *goodness*, He loves you so intimately that He wants to stroll hand in hand with you along the beach of your life. But for God to take your hand, you must first be close, choosing to be within His reach. God doesn't force His hand with you. Draw near to Him so He can reach you.

Don't Worry, I Have You Covered

". . . And says to you, 'Do not fear, I will help you.'" Look what God does: He talks directly to you—it's personal! And look what He says. "Don't be afraid—I *will* help you." He doesn't say, "I *might* help you if you've been a good boy or girl. I *might* help you if you promise to do this or that . . ." No. God says He *will* help. Period. The all-powerful God of the universe says not to be afraid—He has you covered.

This verse paints a picture of a loving parent tenderly grasping the hand of His little one and speaking sweet words of comfort and encouragement. Since you are either a parent and/or someone's child, you've hopefully experienced this on a human level. But have you ever experienced this with your heavenly Father? You don't need your imagination. God and His promises are the real McCoy—take hold of them. He's your God. Let Him take your hand. Listen as He speaks to you. Don't be afraid. Let Him help you.

He's there now, waiting for you. Imagine Him waving you toward Him at the water's edge. Go ahead, draw near to Him. Walk along your life's beach, hand in hand with the One who loves you . . . more than you could ever imagine.

You number my wanderings;
Put my tears into Your bottle.

—Psalm 56:8, NKJV

Chapter 17

MESSAGE IN A BOTTLE

She decides to go for a run. Exercise is great for her body. It is also excellent for her mind. She doesn't know it, but these small details of her life are like props in a big-screen romance, easily recognized by anyone who's survived a loss. Running frees her from thinking about him . . . a love lost from betrayal. The accelerated pace of her heartbeat and of the passing coastal scenery are good for her heart in more ways than one. It feels as though her heart is alive again and growing, rather than moribund from untold hurt.

As she runs along the beach of Cape Cod on this misty day, something catches her eye. Sticking out of the wet sand at the shoreline is a bottle. She stops and gently pulls the bottle from the sand, carefully wiping away its sandy encasement. There is a note inside. She sits down and pulls the cork from the top of the bottle. What she finds there is an incredible, ardent message. It is a message written with more heartfelt longing than she has ever encountered. It is a message of regret for things not done and for words never said.

Sadly, she has learned that internalized, corked-up expressions of regret are not uncommon in many people's lives. But this message is different, both in its passion and its . . . gratitude. Yes, gratitude. She is struck by the note's message of appreciation and profound thanks for a love known. It is simply signed, "*G.*"

She feels that the author of this note has awakened something she has been secretly craving, but that she thought couldn't possibly exist in this cold world. Try as she may, she cannot escape the message in the bottle. She must know who wrote it. She must find this one whose heart touched her own with such honesty, experience, and emotional depth.

So, she begins the search. As a researcher, she knows what to do and where to begin. Eventually she finds the author, a sailboat builder from the Outer Banks of North Carolina. He, too, has a broken heart from a love lost, but his was lost to death. Two broken hearts come back to life again as love's healing process begins.

The scenario above was beautifully depicted in the film *Message in a Bottle*. If only it ended differently. Each time I watch it, I am tearfully swept away with such hope that it will end differently *this* time. If you haven't seen it, I'm not going to spoil it for you. But I will say this—despite the ending, two hearts are healed. Two hearts learned to live again. And those two hearts brought fresh life back to an otherwise dead existence for two lonely souls, all because of a message in a bottle.

Ocean-going bottles are nothing new, nor have they been used just for romantic pining. I found a fascinating history of messages in bottles in a wonderful book, *The Ocean Almanac,* by Robert Hendrickson. Mr. Hendrickson's research is as fascinating as it is broad. It relates the scientific use of floating bottles as early as 310 BC, when a Greek philosopher used them to prove his theory that the Mediterranean was formed by the inflow of the Atlantic. Also noted, from Elizabethan England, is the "Official Uncorker of Ocean Bottles," who had the sole duty of reading messages found in bottles used for espionage and relaying messages to the Admiralty. Hendrickson himself seems amazed at how well this seemingly random method of message-transmission and scientific inquiry has worked: "Fortunes have been made by lucky finders, marriages consummated, rescues made, tragedies disclosed, fishing grounds charted, and currents measured to expedite voyages."[1]

Some of Hendrickson's stories are too good and too pithy not to quote directly. Here are a few of my favorites—it is uncanny what has happened with bottled messages!

> Some years ago, a lucky dishwasher picked up a bottle that the sea had washed ashore. Inside he found a note written 13 years previously which read: "To avoid all confusion, I leave my entire estate to the lucky person who finds this bottle and to my attorney, Barry Cohen, share and share alike." The note was signed Daisy Alexander, daughter of Isaac Singer, the sewing machine tycoon who left a fortune of 12 million dollars . . .
>
> A Florida sailor on shipboard hundreds of miles at sea wrote a

> letter to his wife in Miami and tossed it overboard in a bottle. The bottle washed ashore 20 miles from Miami and was delivered to his wife two days after he had written it . . .
>
> Major Duncan MacGregor described the sinking of the British transport Kent, which Macgregor had survived. Nine years later and 5,000 miles from the scene, the bottle finally washed ashore at the feet of a native servant on Barbados Island who took it to his employer—the same Major MacGregor![2]

Is that wild, or what?! And did you know that Benjamin Franklin used bottles to chart ocean currents—many so accurately that they are followed today by scientists worldwide, including the U.S. Coast and Geodetic Survey?[3] You may even find one of their bottles someday, asking you to return it as part of their ongoing study.

Do you want to know the farthest a bottle has traveled? While much debated, a 1929 German scientific study probably holds the record. As author Hendrickson tells it, "German scientists released a bottle in the South Indian Ocean with a note enclosed asking that it be recorded and thrown back into the sea. It was first reported at Cape Horn. Tossed back, it was found in 1935 off the coast of Australia, a journey of over 16,000 miles."[4]

How about the longest a bottle has bobbed in the ocean? Well, in 1784, a Japanese treasure hunter named Matsuyama was shipwrecked on a Pacific reef. "Before he and his other 44 shipmates perished," Hendrickson tells us, "Matsuyama carved on a small piece of wood an account of their plight and sealed it in a bottle. Almost 150 years later, in 1943, the bottle washed up in the village of his birth."[5]

Isn't it amazing that a vessel of glass and a simple cork can provide such an enduring vehicle for transmission of vital messages all over the world? I wonder which we think is most intriguing—the message, or the bottle and its journey? Perhaps it's only in the combination that we find such wonder. But in the end, it is the message that compels us to act. To claim a treasure, to notify a loved one, to rescue one who is lost, or to record history, we all need to find the author of the message.

Let me restate the verse that began this chapter: "You number my wanderings; put my tears in Your bottle." God knows all about your journey. He knows how long and how far you have wandered in your quest to be found. He knows each current that has carried you to where you are today. God knows the hurt you have experienced—the betrayals, the rejection, the loss, the love you have lost. And God has heard your cries for rescue—from your island of past mistakes, hurt, or utter loneliness. God has heard your longings for peace to replace the turmoil and emptiness in your spirit. God knows you so intimately that He puts your tears in His bottle. God has received your message loud and clear and has responded in kind. In fact, He anticipated your bottled tears and tossed out His own message in a bottle long before you were even born. *God's* message is a map to a true-life treasure, which is waiting for you to seek and claim it.

God originally delivered His message in one vessel, but the message was so tremendous that it has been transcribed and can now be found in numerous vessels. The message has traveled the farthest and the longest, and it lives within jars of clay all over the world.

> "But we have this treasure in jars of clay to show that this all-surpassing power is from God and not from us" (2 Corinthians 4:7, NIV).

What does the Bible mean by "jars of clay?" The jars of clay are imperfect people who have found God's message as well as the Author. They know that it is God's powerful presence within their weak vessels that has made all the difference in their journeys. They have found a love they never knew could exist in this cold world. The message was so heartfelt and filled with a depth of emotion that they had to know the Author. They were compelled to find Him. Once found, the Author provided rescue from the hurt, rescue from the past, and rescue from a hopeless future. He provided an untold treasure of a life eternally filled with love, peace, hope, and joy. He brought fresh life back to an otherwise dead existence for lonely souls—all because of a message in a bottle.

That's a message—and an Author—worth finding, don't you think? Here's the surprising, passionate, just-for-you message:

> "For God so loved the world that he gave his one and only Son, that whoever believes in him shall not perish but have eternal life" (John 3:16, NIV). —*G.*

Now, are you ready to go find the Author?

And God said, "Let the water teem with living creatures,
and let birds fly above the earth across the vault of the sky."
So God created the great creatures of the sea and every living thing
with which the water teems and that moves about in it,
according to their kinds, and every winged bird according
to its kind. And God saw that it was good.

—Genesis 1:20–21, NIV

Chapter 18

GOD'S SANDCASTLE

Have you ever noticed how people act when they are at the beach? It never ceases to amuse me. I especially like to watch the little kids. Their surroundings fill them with such a sense of freedom and joy that anyone watching can see their delight. They mimic funny little sandpipers as they run on tiptoe all along the water's edge. They shout and squeal at the top of their lungs—their "outside voice" is let loose with reckless abandon. Their creativity in designing sandcastles and sand sculptures is a wonderful thing to observe. Armed with an arsenal of plastic sand toys, they can erect an entire sandcastle city in a matter of hours, complete with moats and a fortress of walls. What decorations do the young architects use to ornament their formidable designs? Myriad shells, sea grass, and sticks, placed in askew order—with great seriousness—by little fingers.

And if kids aren't in the mood to build and create, they just play. In the water, in the tide pools, with floats and boogie boards, kids will play for hours on end. Utter freedom. Continual laughter. Open-ended creativity. Unlimited playtime. What a wonderful place for children to experience the heights of childhood!

But as I look around me here on the beach, there's not much difference in how the adults act. Almost everybody acts like a kid. The big people seem to abandon inhibitions as easily as the little ones. They laugh, squeal, run around, swim, jump in the waves, dig in the sand, beachcomb for treasure, fly kites, play Frisbee, read, and even take naps, right out in the open, just as the littlest ones do.

Where does this childlike freedom come from? It's there as soon as you walk from your inland life, climb over that last sand dune, and feel the sea breeze hit your face. What in the world is in that sea breeze anyway?! If only we could bottle its spirit-releasing power and take it home with us. Can you imagine being able to take that bottle to work with you and open it up on especially weary days? Wow—what a boost *that* would be, huh?

Well, whatever is in that sea breeze, it must be extremely powerful because even God seems to have been affected by it. How so? First, because He observed it—along with all His creation—and "saw that it was good," i.e., He *delighted* in it. But I think there's even more obvious proof that the places where land meets sea are high on the list of the Almighty. If you stop and look closely at coastal design and marine life, there exists a wealth of creativity, playfulness, and even humor that boggles the mind. The hugeness of it and the delicacy . . . the simplicity and the complexity . . . God made it all. I can't help but think that something must have put Him in a jazzed mood to lavish so much creativity and attention on coastal life.

If you think my suggestion of a parallel between bare little sandcastle builders and the God of the universe is sacrilegious, please bear with me. Perhaps you've never seen this lighter side of God. If not, let me take you on a little walk along the beach to show you what I mean.

The God Who Loves to Play with the Sand

"How inappropriate to call this planet Earth when clearly it is Ocean."
—*Arthur Clarke*[1]

OK, let's start with the obvious: God liked the ocean so much that He decided to cover 71 percent of the world's surface with it! But He also gave it limits: ". . . This far you may come and no farther; here is where your proud waves halt" (Job 38:11, NIV). Even though He tells each wave exactly how far it can go, He also allows His creation to grow and change like any living thing. Over thousands of years, coastlines recede and expand. What might be covered with water today could be a thriving beachfront community in a few millennia. Or the beach I'm sitting on this afternoon could have a coral reef growing on it in a few centuries.

Not only do waterlines change over time; beaches themselves change—with the seasons as well as daily. Sand-sculpting winds and powerful tides constantly transform the beach topography. In winter, tides are very strong and erosion gives beaches greater slopes into the water.

In summer tides aren't so strong; erosion is less, and the beach has more of a gentle slope. Farther up on land, winds create and build dunes and sand cliffs or "shelves." I've seen this dramatically on St. George Island, Florida. One day there might be a two-to-three-foot sand cliff near the waterline, so sturdy that you can sit on it. The next day, it might be completely gone and flat as a pancake. So, God enjoys creating sand sculptures as well. It never gets old for Him. But He didn't stop with the constantly morphing shapes of the beach; He decided to be creative and even make the sands of different beaches in a rainbow of colors.

My husband, Casey, took me to Barbados for our 11th anniversary. We arrived late at night and could smell the sweet air that was saturated with the scent of bougainvillea. We didn't see the sand until the next morning and was it ever a sight to wake up to—it was pink! We couldn't believe it. Barbados is a coral island, so the sand gets its color from the ground-up coral that makes up the beach. I had to bring some of this beautiful pink sand back with me, so it sits in a bottle in my beach room. Other islands, such as those of Hawaii, have beaches with black, volcanic sand. I'm sad to say I can't give you an eyewitness account on this sand . . . I need to do some primary sand research and get back to you.

Isn't it an interesting characteristic of God, the creative architect? He heaped the wonderful coasts He made with unique designs, shapes, and color. Given the joy so many of us take in this creation of His, I think it's a safe bet that God, too, loves to play in the sand.

The God Who Loves to Decorate

There's a lot more at the beach than just the water and the sand. Just as children decorate their sandcastles, God decorates His project with a seemingly infinite list of living things. He thought things like sea oats, sea grass, wildflowers, morning glories, and palm trees would add just the right touch to bring some greenery to the landscape. But God is also into mobile art, so He created creatures to inhabit the beach and the sea. Some sailors might say that God may have even gone a little overboard—the abundance of coastal and sea life is staggering. "There is the sea, vast and spacious, teeming with creatures beyond number—living things both large and small" (Psalm 104:25, NIV).

I've always been a beachcomber, and love to meander down the beach in search of natural treasure. I'm familiar with many of the creatures I find, but I didn't realize how little I knew and how much I have been overlooking until today. I'm sitting here on Huntington Beach, South Carolina, which is a state park and wildlife reserve. I picked up a copy of *A Peterson First Guide to Seashores,* and it describes over 300 common animals and plants along seashores of North America. I sat down and read this little book, and I feel as though I've seen at least half of these creatures today. Isn't it amazing that you don't always see what you are looking at until you *know* what it is that you are looking at? It doesn't take much sometimes. Just a little knowledge doesn't always have to be a dangerous thing—it can be enlightening.

Let me tell you the treasures I've found today. I'll only give you the highlights: purple sea urchin, orange sea sponge, angel wing shell, green fleece seaweed, common razor clam, lady crab, coquina clams, skate egg case, ghost crab, channeled whelk, northern moon shell, moon jelly, tortoiseshell limpet, Irish moss, rockweed, beach fleas, acorn barnacles, stout tagelus, grass shrimp, and bay scallops. Yes, you too can impress your friends by learning sea-life terminology. But wait! There's more! Here's a list of the birds I've seen today: sanderling, common tern, piping plover, brown pelican, herring gull, osprey, willet, and a long-billed dowitcher. (I know you're just itching to run out and buy a copy of your own *Peterson's* guide to memorize for your next party.)

And guess what I saw evidence of today? There are hundreds of types of marine worms under the sand—clamworms, plumed worms, lugworms, fan worms, bamboo worms, and acorn worms. There also are pinhead-sized and microscopic plants and animals in the sand. Need I go on? *(NO! PLEASE STOP!)* I know, I'd be a dangerous opponent in Trivial Pursuit, Beach Worm Edition.

The point is that God's imagination ran *wild* when He made the coast! He filled it with so much ornamentation and so many occupants that I doubt even the best marine biologist in the world could name them all. New species are continually being discovered. I sometimes wonder if that's because they've never been seen, or if God just never stops creating. Discovery many times requires nothing more than a slower pace. There's no better place to experience that than at the beach. Go beachcomb or sit in a tide pool and just start looking and digging all around—you'll be amazed by what you find.

The God Who Is a Comedian

Another thought blows my mind: What we see on the beach, that which either lives on land or washes ashore, is just the tip of the iceberg out there in that vast ocean. There are sharks, eels, squid, octopuses, lobsters, rays, sea turtles, anemones, kelp beds, manatees, dolphins, whales, plankton, fish, mollusks, starfish, jellyfish, yada, yada, yada. The sea is rich with life; but did you know it is rich with humor?

While we were in Barbados, we went out snorkeling on one of those sailing catamaran cruisers for the day. It was so fun as we dove on a coral reef and on a sunken ship while surrounded by schools of colorful fish. One of the most interesting and funny things we saw was hundreds of flying fish. These fish "flew" alongside us as we cruised along. Let me whip out my *Peterson's* guide here—"Flying fish are silvery, with huge fins that look and act like wings. Flying fish do not actually fly but leap from the sea and glide sometimes up to 100 feet or more"[2] (page 88 for your reference when you get your own copy). Now stop and think about that for a moment. Why in the world would God make a fish that flies? Or a bird that swims? It's just plain funny! Such a spectacle brings delight to its Creator. Humor many times is just the ordinary doing extraordinary things.

OK, what about seahorses? The *males* have the babies. It gives me great satisfaction to know that there is at least one male species out there that knows firsthand what it's like to get fat and give birth. Then there are the entertaining sea lions and sea otters. For our fifth anniversary, we went to California to cruise along the Pacific coast for nine days. My favorite place was undoubtedly Monterey. We rented a kayak and spent a day kayaking over the kelp beds in Monterey Bay. Not only did the awesome beauty of the kelp beds strike us; we were entertained all day by playful sea lions and sea otters. The sea lions popped up all around our kayak, doing flips and playing together.

My *Peterson* guide explains that *(Oh, no— here she goes again!)* "sea lions have small external ears. They often sit upright, looking like dogs with flippers. Males weigh up to 660 pounds and they bark quite loudly."[3] No foolin', Peterson. These sea lions are so loud you can hear them bark from a great distance away. They litter piers in California, soaking up the California sunshine. They look positively dopey on land, but once they are in the water, they are expert swimmers.

But the sea otters are just too cute for words. These fuzzy little creatures have irresistible faces and hang out on their backs on top of the kelp beds. They use rocks to crack open sea urchins or mollusks that they hold on their chests. Think about that. A back-floating Beanie Baby cracking open his lunch on his belly. It was sheer joy to watch their precious behavior as we kayaked among them, often laughing out loud.

The God Who Gives Valentines

Coral reefs decorate tropical waters worldwide in all shapes and sizes. These complex eco-systems are comprised of colonies of tiny animals that provide a rich haven for marine life. Some coral reefs resemble brains; others look like groves of reindeer antlers, just to name a couple. Before I ever had a wonderful husband to take me on trips, I had a wonderful family friend that did.

When I was sixteen, Jack Turney took my family to the island of Bonaire, in the Netherlands Antilles. We had a marvelous time and were blessed to stay in a beautiful home overlooking the bluest sea I've ever seen. The back yard was a coral reef—it was Snorkel City. We saw so many beautiful and funny sights over the grove of reindeer coral there. We kept hearing a crunching sound and discovered it was coming from a Parrotfish munching on the coral with its strong teeth. I wondered if fish have dentists.

While beachcombing at Bonaire, I came across an unusual find. It was a piece of four-inch coral in the perfect shape of a heart. It was sitting around other chunky pieces of coral and certainly wasn't hand carved. It was a God-carved valentine. That valentine also sits in my beach room along with the pink sand and hundreds of other treasures I've collected over the years.

You know what? All of God's creations are valentines—for you and for me. Not only did they bring God delight when He made them, but

He certainly knew they would bring us delight, too. He knew our eyes would widen as we gaped at the beauty we'd see. He knew we'd laugh at the funny quirks in nature and when we saw our own looks or behavior caricatured in that of sea creatures. He knew we would stand in awe of such wonder and incredible architectural design. He made and decorated His big sandcastle to woo us and to show us that the seed and flower of His creation are love.

I hope you will take away two things from this nature documentary. First, stand in awe of how incredible God is! His creativity and humor are unmatched. And consider this: For every species I've mentioned, there is a complete, perfect life cycle of development and an intrinsic role for each creature to play in balancing the ecosystem that sustains the Earth. Many of these creatures come in an array of colors and sizes. God is infinitely interested in the details of each one. Why did He make so many creatures? Because it pleased Him to do so, just for the fun and sheer delight of playing in the sand, and for bringing delight to the faces of His children as they do the same.

For God, creating all these wonderful creatures was *nothing* compared to the pleasure it gave Him to create you. If you think God was jazzed when He made the coast, He was *ecstatic* when He designed you. God talks about us as "sons and daughters." You mean more to Him than all the shells, fish, birds, mammals, and coral combined. He delights simply in your existence and is willing to lavish His attention on every detail of your life. God hears every beat of your heart, and guess what? The sound of that tide is the one He loves best.

God also hears every salty tear that falls from your eyes; He sees every far-off longing of your heart; and He could write a travel guide of every moment that's ever troubled you or brought you delight. I love the way the Psalmist puts it:

> O Lord, you have examined my heart
> and know everything about me.
> You know when I sit down or stand up.
> You know my thoughts even when I'm far away.
> You see me when I travel

and when I rest at home.
    You know everything I do.
You know what I am going to say
    even before I say it, LORD.
You go before me and follow me.
    You place your hand of blessing on my head.
Such knowledge is too wonderful for me,
    too great for me to understand!
I can never escape from your Spirit!

I can never get away from your presence!
If I go up to heaven, you are there;
    if I go down to the grave, you are there.
If I ride the wings of the morning,
    if I dwell by the farthest oceans,
even there your hand will guide me,
    and your strength will support me. . . .
You made all the delicate, inner parts of my body
    and knit me together in my mother's womb.
Thank you for making me so wonderfully complex!
    Your workmanship is marvelous—how well I know it.
You watched me as I was being formed in utter seclusion,
    as I was woven together in the dark of the womb.
You saw me before I was born.
    Every day of my life was recorded in your book.
Every moment was laid out
    before a single day had passed.

How precious are your thoughts about me, O God.
    They cannot be numbered!
I can't even count them;
    they outnumber the grains of sand!
(Psalm 139:1–10, 13–18, NIV)

In order to know where you're going,
you have to know where you've been.

—Mildred Barringer

Chapter 19

SEA TURTLE TRUTHS

For a six-year-old, my son, Alex, has quite an impressive stuffed sea-animal collection, or the "aquarium," as I like to call it. The boy loves sea creatures of all kinds, and he welcomes new additions to his schools (of fish, that is) upon the return of a traveling parent or a special trip to the coast. Each night he sleeps in an ocean of dolphins, sharks, whales, otters, seals, fish, stingrays, walrus, manatees, and of course, "the turtle family."

The turtle family began with a stuffed sea turtle named Teddy—I know, you're thinking bear, but *this* Teddy is a turtle. Teddy came from St. George Island, Florida, where we have a family vacation home, and where sea turtles come to nest. Other turtles have joined the family from different places, but Teddy remains the patriarch.

Sea turtles are amazing creatures. So large, so slow, so beautiful. They are gentle, peaceful, and they gracefully "fly" up to almost six miles per hour, through clear blue waters the whole world over. The different types of sea turtles—Leatherback, Loggerhead, Hawksbill, Ridley, and Black and Green sea turtles—have differing swimming and diving skills. Leatherbacks can dive almost 4,000 feet to find jellyfish. Green sea turtles can stay submerged for nearly five hours as their heart rate slows to conserve oxygen. How perfectly suited these guys are to live and thrive in the sea! But the very attributes that make them thrive in the sea slow them down on land.[1]

Year after year, sea turtles come to nest on the same beach where they were born. No one knows why, or how. The mystery of the sea turtles' annual return has its roots in the distant, unsearchable past. But we can observe their egg-laying process, and it is an incredible thing to see.

During warm months, most female sea turtles come ashore alone during the night when the tide is high. A female sea turtle must use her flippers to dig a nest in which she will lay 50 to 200 eggs. The eggs resemble ping-pong balls. Once she has loosely covered her eggs with sand, the turtle slowly makes her way back to the sea, leaving her spawn to make it on their own.

Sea turtle hatchlings are in danger from natural predators such as crabs, gulls, and raccoons. After emerging from their eggs—soft, helpless, and snack-sized—they immediately look for the sea. Newly born and in the dark, they instinctively know their destination by turning toward the brightest light source, which at night is the ocean. If the hatchlings see lights from houses along a beach, they can become disoriented and go deeper into predator territory.[2]

When they make it to the sea—*if* they do—hatchlings remain in danger as they grow. They can get caught in fishing nets or be hunted by humans for their meat, eggs, leather, and shells. The world has finally awakened to the fact that sea turtles are endangered, and international measures to protect them have been put into place. I hope it will not be too late to save one of God's most unique creatures. They are wise little sea gems the generations of which offer much more than what a hunter seeks.

So, what wisdom did God instill in the sea turtle for us to see? Well, it might be to just simply slow down. One of my favorite tee shirts says, "Sail fast, live slow." I'm sure that's a guide with which any sea turtle would agree. I think turtles see much more on their trips than we do on ours. Funny how that works. When you slow the pace, you see things that were always there but were never visible to the hurried, distracted eye. As I said before about beachcombing, discovery can be so exciting and often doesn't require anything more than a slower pace.

Another thing we can learn from these graceful creatures is just that—grace. Live it—extend it to others in your actions. Be gentle. Be kind. Don't seek to offend any but to enlighten all. Fly as you were made to do when you are in your element. And for those times when you are out of your element on the sand, be graceful on the inside anyway. You may appear slow and clumsy on the outside, but you were put here for a purpose. Let nothing stop you. Pursue your mission until it is accomplished.

Then glide back into your element, confident that you achieved what you set out to do.

Perhaps the most important thing the sea turtle has taught me is to remember my roots and to go back to them frequently. I have been blessed with generations of family with an instinct for returning to the important places in life. My grandmother was a walking book of wisdom. I enjoyed listening to her life helps from a child to an adult. She repeated them often, and for that I am grateful. They're easy to remember because I understand the tremendous value they hold. One of her classic statements has always been "In order to know where you're going, you have to know where you've been."

It's a saying so simple, but so profound, that it's worth repeating. *In order to know where you're going, you have to know where you've been.* It seems we've learned another lesson from the sea turtles: repeat what works, and your children and grandchildren will have an easier task finding their way.

What does Grandmother's nugget mean? Well, know your roots—know your family history, and be honest about your personal history. Whether your background is one of which to be proud, or one that brings shame—*know* it. Once you understand your starting point, you can begin to chart your course. You may choose to stay on the same tack if that starting point was one of goodness and light, or if the starting point was one of heartache and pain, you may choose to alter your course and leave a new, better starting point for *your* children. Just as a navigating sailor takes position measurements on nautical charts to track his course, we can do the same in our life journey. Charting your course is important.

Not only do sailors chart locations on a map, but they also log conditions along the way—winds, tides, water depths, observations, etc. I have long kept a daily journal to log life events along my journey. Most of the time it is filled with just the normal, daily activities. But when the tough or joyful experiences come along, it is a wonderful, healthy practice to have a record of how the experience began, how God worked the circumstances together for good, and what was the result. It is a great feeling to be able to go back and read the conditions of previous storms to gain insight into weathering new ones. And what a treasure to leave your children—a well-documented chart of their family's journey.

Isn't it interesting that just as the sea turtle is endangered, so too is the content of the wisdom he imparts? In our fast-paced world, the qualities of living slowly, living gracefully, and returning to your roots seem all too often endangered. I hope that our respect, protection, and care for the sea turtle will grow. I hope that people in the future continue to find ways to slow down, to act with grace, and to remember and reflect. And I hope that when Alex outgrows Teddy, he will retain the wisdom of the gentle, wise sea turtle that his cuddly friend symbolizes.

Do not forget to entertain strangers,
for by so doing some have
unwittingly entertained angels.

—Hebrews 13:2, NKJV

Chapter 20

ANGELS OF THE SEA

Waverunner Waywardness

I have a confession to make. I haven't been totally honest with you. After all my accolades on the virtues of sailing, it's time I told you something. I became a gnat years ago. Our family got a new toy—a Yamaha Waverunner—and I fell for it hook, line, and sinker.

These are the evil watercraft that wreak havoc with the serenity of sailing. The sound is obnoxious, the fumes are annoying, and the wake bumps sailboats that are either calmly anchored or enjoying a peaceful sail. The last thing a sailor wants to hear or see is an irritating, gas-fuming gnat of a Waverunner.

Gnats tend to chase the wakes of other boats to jump the waves, hence the endearing name. I really can't help my gnatitis—these things are *so* fun! I love to ride at top speed, jumping some waves, riding the crests of others, and getting drenched in the process. It is a *blast* to ride parallel to the beach on ocean waves. I've been tempted more than once to head out to the open sea just to go there. But, unlike a sailboat that can come back under sail, I'd run out of gas eventually on the Waverunner.

Once in Myrtle Beach my dad panicked, as I appeared to be doing just that. I went out so far that he could barely see me from the shore. He just knew that I was going to meet Jaws in person. He is plagued with that picture in his mind and still talks today about how I graciously gave him a near heart attack. (Sorry, Dad.)

Dolphin Quest

When I, the gnat, was out so far in the ocean, I was looking for some friends: dolphins. I always look for them out in the water. These creatures are very dear to me, as they are to many people. Yes, "Flipper" had a profound impact on my generation. What kid didn't wish he or she could be Bud and have Flipper as a pet?

If you've ever been to the dolphin show at Sea World, there is always standing room only. Have you ever wondered why people love dolphins? What is it about them that appeals to us? Is it their gentle nature? Their playful antics? Their remarkable intelligence? Or is it "all of the above"?

Dolphins have been revered and respected since time began. They have adorned important cultural objects such as coins, pottery, and paintings. They are woven through pages of time in Greek and Roman mythology. In many Greek legends, the gods, particularly Apollo, took the form of a dolphin. The word "dolphin" has its origins in the classical Greek word *delphis*, which means "womb," or the beginning of life.[1]

Throughout history there have been countless stories of how dolphins have saved people lost at sea. As early as 2,700 years ago, a Greek poet named Arion is said to have been saved from the sea by a dolphin after he was thrown overboard by sailors.[2] And in 1999, a young six-year-old boy named Elian was helped by dolphins when adrift alone at sea. Dolphins fight off sharks and buoy stranded people until help arrives. What an amazing thing; these wonderful creatures go to great lengths to protect those unlike themselves.

Dolphins enjoy human interaction. They will swim around divers and prod them along as if to say, "Let's play!" They also seem to love human interaction by boat. Dolphins frequently follow ships and sailboats as they cruise along. It's as if a man-made vessel is an attempt for man to "join the pod," and they warmly welcome us.

One of my favorite memories was when a pod of dolphins came alongside us while on *Agape* in the Florida Keys. We were heading into Key Largo to anchor, and two dolphins were literally hugging the bow of the boat. I was eager to get anchored so I could jump over and swim with them. But as we dropped anchor, the dolphins disappeared, as did my hope of joining them. I have always longed to swim with these elusive guys. It's been on my "life to-do list" to get checked off eventually.

Another night we were anchored in a cove, and I was sleeping out in the cockpit under a blanket of stars. Several dolphins surfaced around the boat, and the only sound was that of exhaling blowholes. It was a beautiful, peaceful sound, knowing that these mammals were surrounding *Agape* in the dark of night. What a wonderful feeling of protection!

Whether I am on the boat or at the beach, my eye is constantly roving the waters for an emerging dorsal fin belonging to a dolphin. St. George Island has a tremendous population of wild dolphin, which grace shallow waters right off the beach. I have never seen dolphins so active in the wild as I have there. They jump clear out of the water, slap their tails on the surface, and literally surf in the waves. They are self-contained surfboards! They have freedom and an exuberance of which I cannot get enough.

I long ago gave up trying to swim out to them as they cruise by. Maybe they know that I'm not in trouble and need help. Maybe they know that I'm not equipped with scuba gear to get underwater and play with them. Whatever the curious reason, they keep their distance. With their superior sonar they can see *me* fine when they disappear from my sight. They hear every breath I take and know every move I make. So, I hop on the Waverunner and go out to deeper water where they are, following stingrays coasting under me.

Out past the sandbar, dolphins swim all around me! I can't tell you how fun this is. They seem to enjoy popping up behind me in a hide-and-seek game. Once, a baby dolphin swam belly-up, brushing underneath the Waverunner. If I keep my obnoxious motor on, they stay. The minute I turn it off, they vanish. Go figure.

I love this interaction, but at the same time it is frustrating to be so close yet so far away in terms of making physical contact. Why do they choose to interact with us in some situations, yet remain so elusive in others? My frustration has been somewhat assuaged by visiting Sea World, where you can touch and feed dolphins in a beautiful cove-like habitat. You can get up close and personal with a $3.00 carton of smelly fish. Sometimes they will even jump right in front of you to cool you off and ruin your camera.

The "Eyes" Have It

During one of these hands-on encounters, I discovered what it is about dolphins that most appeals to me. Oddly enough, it's the same thing that most appeals to me about people. It's the eyes. As I was feeding the dolphins, one came up close beside me, and we made eye contact. There was something very soulful and penetrating about those dolphin eyes. They reflected warmth, wisdom, knowledge, and . . . a mysterious feeling of understanding. This encounter was during the midst of my category 2 storm when I was so sad. Could this dolphin read my emotions? I truly felt as if he saw *something* as he floated there next to me, and it wasn't just the smelly fish in my hand. His smiling gaze brought a smile to my face and to my heart.

I am an eye studier. You can tell much about what is in a person's heart by looking into their eyes. You can see not only into their current emotional state but also into their entire lifetime of experience. Lives of joy produce naturally smiling eyes. Lives of pain produce burdened eyes. Whatever the emotion of the moment—love, anger, disinterest, enthusiasm, sadness, happiness—the lifetime eyes tell the real story.

Clearly something substantial lies behind the eyes of a dolphin, much different than those of just a simple fish. Have you ever looked at the eyes of a fish? There's nothing there, just a blank existence. Next time you're at the grocery store, go look at the fresh fish section with row on row of blank eyes. "Well, *duh* Jenny. Of course, they are blank. They're all dead!" Work with me here—there's a method to my madness. OK, next time you see a *live* fish, look at the eyes. The live ones look just as blank in the eyes as the dead ones.

Scientists have studied dolphins and learned that they are incredibly intelligent mammals. They actually are small whales, of which there are thirty-three known species of ocean dolphins, five river dolphins, and six kinds of porpoise. The Bottlenose Dolphin is probably the most well-known and is the largest of the "beaked" dolphins. These guys can grow to roughly 12 feet and weigh as much as 800 pounds.[3] I've heard it said that dolphins could even be smarter than humans. Sometimes, I think that wouldn't be much of a stretch, given much of man's behavior today.

The behavior that dolphins exhibit toward family members exudes love and genuine concern. For instance, when a baby dolphin is born, one dolphin helps the calf up to the surface for air while another one remains with the mother to help her recoup from the birth. Such beautiful concern for their own!

But I think it goes deeper than intelligence. Eyes reveal what's in the heart, not the brain. I'm going to pose a theory that is fantasy and total conjecture with absolutely zero biblical foundation whatsoever. Ready? I sometimes wonder if dolphins are the angels of the sea. Think about it. They possess many angelic qualities. Dolphins are protectors. They guard human life in the most unusual circumstances. Why? They travel with humans, always staying close by, even though we can't always see them. Why? They are full of joy, and their playful behavior paints a perfect picture of God's intent for living life to the fullest and having *fun* while doing so. And they are messengers, with those deep, soulful eyes and smiling mouths.

The Message

The message they bring is threefold. The first part of the message is that we should all appeal to the better angels of our nature. Dolphins go out of their way, sometimes at their own risk, to protect humans: total strangers who are not like them in the least. When is the last time you reached out to help someone in a precarious situation, especially someone totally unlike yourself? When was the last time you simply buoyed someone until help arrived?

We don't encounter people in life and death situations very often, but we do encounter people swimming in dangerous life waters every day. Some people need help on a basic level: food, clothing, shelter, or physical assistance from illness or injury. Others are in dangerous emotional waters: a seasick marriage, a marooned family relationship or friendship, a leaking vessel from poor decision-making or from a sheer lack of encouragement. You certainly don't have to look very far. But to be of help, you have to look first.

Open your eyes and your heart to those who need help. It will involve an output of resources of your time, your money, or your emotions. And yes, sometimes it will be risky when the emotional sharks close in, but you can handle them. But please don't try to save *everyone* out there. You'd start quickly sinking yourself. Know when to be elusive and allow someone else to bear the load. Whatever you do, though, don't always remain in calm, safe, isolated waters. Without reaching out, you won't fully grasp the second part of the message.

The second part is this: Keep a smile on your face! Dolphins look that way all the time with that curved mouth of theirs. We, however, have a choice of how to make ours look. We can smile, or we can frown. The smile we choose should not just be surface level, but should spring from the joy deep within: the joy of knowing you have a secure faith; the joy of knowing you are unconditionally loved by the One who made you; the joy of swimming in dangerous waters to help those in need; the joy of just loving life and milking it for all it's worth. Once you have that kind of joy, you'll want to be playful all the time, too, jumping, swimming belly-up, and surfing the waves of happiness. What a terrific message!

The third part of the message is to look deep inside every heart through the window of the eyes. You will see more than you expected. You will be much slower to judge, and much quicker to generate compassion and love. Looking into another's eyes affords communication of the spirit.

People don't act the way they do just to act that way. An emotional undercurrent always drives behavior. If you can try to determine the type of undercurrent, you can better understand why someone is acting in a certain way. Then you can better relate and communicate verbally, whether it be a positive or a negative undercurrent. Hey, I'm no expert. I certainly don't do this as I should. But we would all get along better with each other if we took the time to start with the eyes.

I have noticed an unmistakable quality of eyes that belong to people whose God-shaped voids are filled. Their eyes express joy, peace, love, and kindness greater than human nature—because a nature greater than human resides within. I feel immediate kinship with such eyes. I look forward to the day when I will gaze into the eyes of the One who created that kinship. Those eyes that see deep into my spirit and know my every thought and emotion. Those eyes that share every tear and every laugh along the way. Those eyes that know all there is to know about me and continue to love me anyway. As the song goes, I want to have "my Father's eyes."

Do you have your Father's eyes? Those that are full of life and love that comes from a secure peace deep within? Or are your eyes as blank as that of a simple fish, dead to the love and grace that waits to capture your heart? When God fills your heart, He gives you His eyes as well.

Since God is the Father of all creation, I think He chose to give the dolphin His eyes, or at least the eyes of an angelic messenger of the sea. If He could make a donkey talk (Numbers 22:28), why couldn't He make a dolphin see? Look at the eyes of a dolphin a little differently when you next see one. Whether or not there is any substance to my angelic sea theory, I hope you'll be reminded of your Father's eyes, and how they watch over you . . . and utterly adore you.

When Irish Eyes Are Smiling

The time finally came. On June 17, 2000, I got to swim in the North Atlantic Ocean in Dingle Bay, Ireland, with a dolphin . . . named Fungie. He is a resident dolphin who adopted this scenic harbor in 1983. His presence is highly unusual, since very few dolphins ever venture into Dingle harbor, which is relatively shallow. It was the local fishermen who first noticed Fungie, as he would follow along behind their fishing boats.

The stories of Fungie's antics are numerous and humorous. Sean Mannion authored a book entitled, *Fungie: Ireland's Friendly Dolphin.* In this book he tells some incredible stories about Ireland's angel of the sea. One fisherman recalled a time when he and his son were going out salmon fishing when they saw Fungie jumping like crazy. The fisherman stuck his head out the window to see him, and Fungie jumped up right below his head, knocking the pipe out of his mouth with his belly.[4] Another fisherman and his son were hauling lobster pots early one morning when Fungie jumped over the middle of the boat, right over their heads.[5] And still another fisherman there once remarked, "He was a character. You couldn't come in or out of the harbor without seeing the dolphin's head as high as the level of the wheelhouse window, as if he was trying to look in at you."[6]

But it was the Dingle lighthouseman, Paddy Ferriter, who knew Fungie best. Fungie befriended the old lighthouse keeper when the lone dolphin decided to make a cove called Gravelly Cuas his home. Paddy once recalled the first time he saw the dolphin. "About noon one day I happened to be at the wall outside the lighthouse. I heard a blowing sound, looked around and saw a dolphin in the water just below the lighthouse. I took no special notice of him; I'd seen dolphins before. I went in, had tea, and came out again. He was still there. I remember saying to him, 'You look like a bloke that's going to put down your moorings here for the night.'" Paddy was surprised when Fungie was there again the next day and every day since.[7]

Paddy was witness to Fungie's exploits in discovering his new home, encountering humans, other sea life, and inanimate objects with great curiosity. Fungie appears to have a tremendous need to touch everything he sees. Paddy would often see Fungie playing with the cormorant sea birds. "I remember one poor cormorant trying to swim ashore and Fungie pushing it down time after time. The cormorant made it to shore but that finished them as far as I was concerned. I thought Fungie had malice for them. Then one day I saw something on the lad's back. I got out my spyglass and saw it was a cormorant. Its wings were spread for balance as Fungie moved slowly forward. Then the dolphin just turned on its side and the cormorant slipped into the water."[8]

Fungie was often Paddy's only company. So, this old fisherman watched him daily from the shore in his Irish fisherman sweater, pipe in mouth. Their daily eye contact afforded a growing acquaintance, which grew to increasing familiarity, and friendship for two lone souls. Dolphins mate for life, and the local people have wondered what happened to Fungie's mate. Why did he remain alone? No one really knows for sure. What is known for sure is that Fungie loves Dingle Bay, which has become his soulmate.

His popularity grew in the late 1980's when he became a worldwide celebrity, featured on TV programs and newspapers, including *The Washington Post* and *The New York Times.* One of the funniest stories I read about Fungie concerned a pair of BBC photographers, making a film about him. They were diving around him and wanted to shoot Fungie eating some squid. They held the squid in their hands and waved it in front of Fungie, who wasn't very interested. Finally, the divers acted as if they were eating the squid, and Fungie, seemingly more out of a desire to appear a good dinner guest, accepted some and swam away. The next time the divers saw Fungie, he brought *them* squid to eat, as if to say, "I know you guys really love this stuff, so here you go!"

Fungie welcomes boats coming in and out of the harbor with his characteristically joyful jumps alongside vessels of all shapes and sizes. Fungie once even assisted a small boat that had broken down. According to a local waterman, "There was a young lad in a small punt out in the harbor. His outboard engine cut out and wouldn't restart so he tried to row for shore. He was cutting across the tide, so it wasn't easy. Fungie was up with us but then set off towards the boat. The next thing we saw he was up at the boat's stern pushing against it with his nose. He pushed him for a hundred yards across the tide. The lad in the boat never once realized why the rowing had become easier!"[9]

Fungie also enjoys swimming with people if he's in the mood. So, I boarded an ocean vessel, donned a wetsuit and was eager to meet this 13-foot, 500-pound, beautiful creature. On our way to anchor in a shallow cove, Fungie appeared, and my heart leapt. He followed us into anchor but then turned back to the harbor. The seamen took an outboard Zodiak (sounds like a gnat) out to "get" Fungie and bring him chasing the wake back to the cove. Fungie was at first preoccupied with other matters like a school of fish, and teased us for about an hour, coming near and then leaving. Fungie must be a sailor, as he kept leaving us so he could escort sailboats into the harbor.

I became frustrated so asked if I could jump on the Zodiak to go get Fungie. The Irish seaman pulled me out of the cold water and off we went to find Fungie. It didn't take very long. He came to us. I called out to him, "Come on, Fungie! *I'm* a sailor—come play with me, pal!" He swam under my neon green flippers that I was slapping on the water. He was enormous, and gray, and right there.

I am the queen of persistence and rarely give up my effort to attain something worthwhile. I think Fungie sensed my persistence and followed us back into the cove. This was a gift because Fungie is wild and can do whatever he pleases. He is also annually bombarded with tens of thousands of people who seek him out daily. I respect his right to be alone when he desires and his choice to interact when he desires. So, as we entered the cove, I jumped in, and he decided to stay a little while. I put my mask on and looked underwater, and there he was, right beside me. His smiling Irish eyes looked at me and seemed to say, "Welcome to my world. Or in the Irish Gaelic, *Cead Mile Failte*, meaning a hundred thousand welcomes. You can check this off your life to-do list now. I'm so happy I was the one. And oh, Father sends His love."

It was an experience I will never forget. Thanks, Fungie, my new friend . . . and my angel of the sea. And thanks, God, for giving me the desire of my heart.

As long as I remain a gnat, I will be thankful that I have two sets of "Father eyes" watching me from above and from the shore. And perhaps a pair watching from beneath the waves as well.

To try to understand the real significance of what the great artists, the serious masters, tell us in their masterpieces that lead to God; one man wrote or told it in a book, another in a picture.

—Vincent Van Gogh[1]

Chapter 21

THE LONELY PAINTER AND THE SEA

A Living Canvas

En somme, trois choses demeurent : la foi, l'espérance et l'amour, mais la plus grande d'entre elles, c'est l'amour.

Pardon my French—I'll translate in a minute.

I simply adore the French language. It has been called the language of love, and I can see why. I love to hear it. I love to speak it . . . well, attempt to speak it. I'm slowly learning but still elicit smiles from French waiters when I butcher the language. I appreciate how they graciously begin to speak English when they realize I'm a well-meaning American who is way in over my verbally challenged head.

But it's not just the language that captivates me; I simply adore *everything* French—the cuisine, the scenery, the people, the history, (and OK, not their politics), but of course, the art. After roaming Paris, the coasts, and the countryside in France, I imagine that I've partaken in a small way the unbelievable beauty that inspired Monet, Renoir, Gauguin, Van Gogh, and many other painters. I strolled through Monet's private gardens and walked over that now world-famous little bridge that spans his water garden, brimming with lilies. Then I stood in the *Musée d'Orsay* in Paris and gaped at Monet's work hung in great halls of splendor. I thought, "He totally and completely captured the essence of what he saw." When it comes to serene beauty captured on canvas, *Monet est magnifique!*

But it is Van Gogh who has most captured me with the canvas of his life behind the art. I recently spent some time in Provence in the south of France. While there I followed Vincent Van Gogh around, and I saw the vantage points from which were born his greatest works. I stayed in St.

Remy and gazed at the night sky above the town that Vincent painted into *Starry Night*. I walked through groves of olive trees that Vincent captured as if to empathize with their twisted branches and roots. I stood at the riverfront in Arles where he sat and studied a curve in the riverbank for six months before painting *Arles at Night*. I gazed out the window of Vincent's room in a psychiatric hospital overlooking fields of lavender. But my favorite spot in Vincent's sojourn was a small fishing village overlooking the Mediterranean Sea—Saintes Maries de la Mer.

It was here by the sea that Vincent's artistic spirit came alive. Here he finally came to know that his calling as an artist was true. His self-confidence emerged to make him a great painter. Years of anguish, broken dreams, and love lost had led him on a never-ending quest to find self-worth and value. But sitting by the sea, as he wrote, "on a sandy beach, small green, red, blue boats with such pretty colors that you are reminded of flowers . . ."[2] Vincent breathed in the salt air of the sea, and the liberating air of purpose.

Just as brushstrokes come together on a canvas to create a picture, many brushstrokes of life experiences come together to create a living canvas of who we are.

The Lonely Painter

You've probably heard that Van Gogh's story is a tragic one. He was born into strict and austere beginnings in Holland, the eldest of six children. The son of a country parson, Vincent often heard the words of Jesus, which struck a chord in this highly sensitive boy that he made it his personal mission to help the poor and needy. As a young man, his heart's desire was to be a preacher like his father. Proving his devotion through what he saw as an act of profound obedience to Christ's teaching, Vincent gave up all he had to live in poverty with people he longed to help. It wasn't long before the religious leaders and even his own family rejected Vincent's ways, saying he was a "spiritual agitator."[3] Vincent felt like a failure: a failure before his family, his religious community, and his God. You could say that Vincent's life canvas began with a dark background.

But Vincent's drive to be of use to God didn't end there. In 1880, he decided to become an artist and serve God with his paintbrush. That's when he wrote, "To try to understand the real significance of what the great artists, the serious masters, tell us in their masterpieces, that lead to God; one man wrote or told it in a book; another, in a picture."

Sadly, Vincent's fervor was dampened following another brushstroke of rejection—this time from the woman he loved. He never recovered from this heartbreak and would never know that type of romantic love again. His palette reflected his life experience to date—dark, somber, and lonely. He would paint this way without much success for six years, moving from place to place in search of what was missing.

It was late in this period of his life, in 1885, that Vincent painted *The Potato Eaters.* Later considered his first masterpiece, the painting portrays a poor, peasant family gathered around a table for their daily meal of potatoes and tea. The thick, black outlines of their bodies and the dark, heavily brown palette, used in both their faces and their humble surroundings, clearly communicate the family's weariness. Yet, the subjects are arranged so solemnly around the table that many viewers see in this meal a kind of spiritual ritual or communion. Van Gogh clearly wanted to suggest a spark of holiness amid the most mundane activities: He provides the family with a single gas lamp by which they see and are seen. The lamp, hanging slightly above them, is the focal point of the painting. Its flame of wild yellow is the only unoppressive color in the whole scene. For Van Gogh, this lamp may have had echoes of Jesus ("the light of the world"). Without a doubt it represents hope for something better, a faith in some higher love.

His artistic quest eventually led him to join his brother, Theo, in Paris in 1886. Theo loved Vincent and always gave him unconditional love and financial support as he pursued his dream. Vincent began to learn about a new style of painting called impressionism. It was a revolution! Observing the seemingly careless brushwork of Monet and the others, Vincent realized that he had been the careless one, that he had been preoccupied with painting what was within him, while the French had found a way to free their eyes and paint the world as the light truly falls on it. The dark shades of Vincent's palette became bright with color even as his lingering doubts and depression—the darkness in the palette of his soul—remained.

Ever trying to be of service and worth in his world, yet never seeming to come out from under the mantle of rejection, Vincent spiraled down further and drank heavily, complicating his depression. The brushstrokes on his life canvas became wild and erratic. He had to get out of Paris—away from the lifestyle and the people who continually brought him down. Theo suggested he go to the sunny south of France, so in the cold of winter 1888, Vincent left for Arles to stay in the "yellow house" that his paintings would someday make famous. Arles was to be a chapter with many painful moments, but it yielded one very bright brushstroke of fresh color on Vincent's life canvas.

In early June of that year, he decided to go to the sea. He took a stagecoach through the grass plains of the Camargue down to the coast, to the town of Saintes Maries de la Mer. Here he stayed only a week, but what a difference it made in his life. In that short time, he produced no fewer than three paintings and nine drawings. He left with the confidence that his work would finally be a success.

I'm not going to tell you that Vincent's life was all rosy after he found his calling here—it wasn't. In fact, it got worse as his mental illness intensified. But during it all, an amazing thing happened. As his depression consumed him in the coming two years, Vincent's work blossomed into greatness. He achieved what he had desired for so long—to be a great artist. His newfound confidence and the love of his brother, Theo, kept him going for a time, but it was not enough. Vincent lost all hope and couldn't go on. Taking his life at the age of thirty-seven, he lost a physical battle with mental illness and depression.

How it breaks my heart to think of the years and numerous works Van Gogh could have enjoyed if he could have been helped by the medicines of today. But when I look back to the beginning of his story, to the blank canvas of Vincent's life, I see the beginnings of his depression stemming from brushstrokes of rejection and loneliness. I see an ache in his heart for love and self-worth that launched him down a difficult path, a never-ending pilgrimage to find purpose.

A Gallery of Emotions

After walking in Vincent's footsteps in Provence, I later sat in a chair at the gallery of *Musée d'Orsay* in Paris where many of Vincent's paintings reside today. I sat there for a long time and studied one of his many self-portraits. I sat so long, in fact, that I lost track of time as well as my party, who left me there to go people-watch at a sidewalk café overlooking the Seine. But I just couldn't pull myself away from that tormented face surrounded by swirls of blue. I was immersed in the tragedy of the artist and blown away by the fantastic genius of what this wounded man created.

Look at what drove him. He had a burning desire to serve God. He had faith in God and tried to live it out in the service of others. But those "of the faith" struck him down and made him feel worthless. So, Vincent held on to a hope—a hope that he could be of service to God in another way—through his paintbrush. And that hope was affirmed by a trip to the sea.

I'd like to think that Van Gogh had a spirit like mine—that it was at the sea where his soul encountered God, who opened the painter's eyes to the possibilities of what he could become and accomplish, because he went on from his encounter there to produce the great works we treasure today. You know what I think? As God lovingly looked at Vincent and the coming mental storm he was to endure, I think He graced him with the gifts of confidence and true skill in painting as a haven. Vincent's painting would become a haven. Here he could enter a beautiful world. Here he could know some peace for a time. Here he could feel valuable and feel a sense of accomplishment despite the chaos of his reality. It was finally an answer to Vincent's prayer. God graced Vincent for *Vincent's* sake.

On a human scale, it was the love of his brother, Theo, that kept Vincent going. He never really knew much love from people during his lifetime—not from the religious, not from his romantic interests, not from his colleagues. But Theo never stopped encouraging, supporting, and loving his brother. That love took Vincent far. But oh, to think of how much further he could have gone if those in the faith had dispensed that kind of love to him! I can't help but wonder if a lack of love from the religious translated to him as a lack of love from God. That's the true tragedy here.

Ah, the power of love—or lack thereof. Vincent isn't the only one who has suffered from the lack of it in religious circles. Too many have.

I think that a lack of love among those who profess to have faith has done more to turn people away from God than anything. When those who profess God don't live out His message of love, people are made to feel devalued and unworthy of the supreme love of God.

A Gypsy Spirit

Van Gogh also isn't the only one who has traveled to Saintes Maries de la Mer in search of meaning and direction. Religious pilgrims have traveled to this seaside village for centuries in a quest for a blessing of love and forgiveness. This town is a haven for gypsies whose ancestors as early as the 15th century were "condemned to wander all the world in expiation of their sins."[4] Gypsies are nomads who are not warmly welcomed in churches across Europe, but here it is different. Here they gather en masse and identify with kindred spirits. They come to Saintes Maries de la Mer to offer penance and make vows to the saints Marie-Jacobe and Marie-Salome. Each May they come here for a huge observance of rituals that end with a walk to the sea for a "blessing of the sea."

There is an ancient legend of Saintes Maries de la Mer that has been passed down for centuries. It is said that in 40 A.D., these Marys mentioned frequently in the Bible were victims of Jewish persecution in Jerusalem. So, they and others (Lazarus, Martha, and a servant girl, Sarah) got in a boat (one with no oars or sails, mind you) and drifted across the Mediterranean to land on the shores of this seaside town in the south of France. Here they came to spread the Gospel.

I've found many such legends and relics throughout France. I've been to Chartres and seen Jesus' swaddling clothes encased in a shrine of the old cathedral. I've climbed the steep steps of the city of Rocamadour where tradition holds that Zaccheus came (when he was about 1,000 years old) and brought a carving of the virgin. I've been to the magnificent Mont St. Michel, where God inspired a monk to build a cathedral in the middle of nowhere by laying waste to a forest, clearing the land, and surrounding it with tidal currents.

Hey, I don't put God in a box. He can do anything He wants, and sometimes, I know, He does the unusual. But when I ponder the emergence of all these legends, I see something much greater than simple economic motivation—trade in lore and holy trinkets—which no doubt plays some part in the history of many pilgrimage sites. I have come to believe that the people in these towns—and the pilgrims they attract—have an aching desire to exhibit value and self-worth through tangible religious artifacts or through hearing about the encounters of those who were in the presence of Christ. After all, without this deep desire, what else would draw so many people with so much zeal for so many years? I hear in these stories a plea to God that says, "Please look on us with favor and give us your blessing, love, and approval." Thousands of pilgrims go to these places to participate in the plea. "Please, give me favor, bless me with love for having traveled so far to this holy place. If you can't love me just for me, can you love me for doing something important?"

Be honest: The hunger for love infects each one of us. You may look at the French coastal legends and pilgrimages and dismiss them as strange, but let's look at our own lives. We all look for love on a human level, but ultimately, that's not the love we pursue from the core of our being. The love we seek is at the heart of our existence. It is bound up in our reason for living—our purpose.

Don't we all ache and go on pilgrimages to find supreme love? We might not go in search of tangible religious artifacts, but there are plenty of other ways we look for it. We look for love in our work, in romantic encounters, in power and possessions, and in various life experiences. But the love we seek is not in a place or a person or an experience. It cannot be attained through what we do or how worthy we try to become. How hard we make it on ourselves! And, tragically, how hard we make it on others in the process of our search.

What did Van Gogh do? Through many stormy times, he remained true to the love that was his purpose, his reason for being. By human standards most would call him a failure, an unemployable mental patient, kept afloat by the generosity of his brother. But it doesn't take great spiritual insight to see that Vincent was blessed with a love great enough to create extraordinary beauty. The love we seek requires nothing more than to be true to our innermost selves, which, as Vincent knew, are gifts from God.

The love we seek doesn't require a pilgrimage, for it is with us wherever we are at any given moment. The love we seek cannot be earned through works or sacrifice or anything we can do, save one thing. The love we seek needs only to be received as the gift it was designed to be.

That's it. Open the gift, and it dwells in your heart and your soul. The need to go, see, and do evaporates once you grasp the gift. This love brings to light the self-worth you've had all along. For your purpose is to be loved and held, valuable beyond measure.

La Foi, L'Espérance et L'Amour

Let me translate that French for you now:

> "And now three remain: faith, hope and love. But the greatest of these is love" (1 Corinthians 13:13, NIV).

Now do you see? We can have *faith*, believing in God, and in His word, and in His truth, and that is great. We can have *hope,* as we live life, that God will guide us and bless us, and that, too, is great. But above it all, if we don't accept love—God's supreme love—which fills our souls with self-worth and a reason for being, we miss the greatest thing of all. We were made to be loved by God; we were wired to receive His supreme love. No wonder we ache for it so.

You can't make God love you any more or less. Your worth in His eyes couldn't possibly be greater. He knows a masterpiece when He sees one. God desires for those who have received His supreme love to become conduits of that love. People are looking at the life canvas of those who claim to have the brushstrokes of faith and hope in God. But what they are really searching for are the brushstrokes of supreme love. It's *love* that completes the picture.

If I espouse faith in Christ Jesus on Sunday and yet berate the person who crosses me on Monday, what good is my faith? If I have hope in the grace of God to forgive me for the terrible thing I did on Tuesday, yet refuse to extend love and forgiveness to a hurting soul on Wednesday, what good is my hope? Faith and hope go nowhere without the love because love is why they remain in the first place.

How will those without faith or hope ever come to experience these remaining things if they don't experience the love and grace of God expressed by those of us who claim to have it? How will the Van Goghs of the world ever know they are worthy because of *whose* they are, not because of what they've accomplished? Imagine the beautiful life canvas that can emerge when they know they are loved!

It's love that disarms an angry soul, especially when it seems undeserved. It's love that breaks through walls of hardheartedness when a soul appears to be hopelessly lost. It's love that turns a spiritual gypsy into a secure resident of grace. It's love that brings a shy, lonely soul to blossom and grow in the warmth of its light. It's love that shows to all who see it the nature of God, the direct accessibility to God, and the ultimate desire of God. It's love that leads to faith. It's love that leads to hope. No wonder it remains the greatest.

A Picture Paints Three Words

As you enter the town of Saintes Maries de la Mer, you are greeted by an enormous cast-iron emblem of a cross, anchor, and heart intertwined together. The Camargue Cross is a picture of our verse from First Corinthians. It is a beautiful picture of faith (cross), hope (anchor), and love (heart.) That image grabbed me from the moment I saw it, and it now graces the pages of this book.

As I walked along the beach at Saintes Maries de la Mer, I pondered what this town's emblem means. I thought about Vincent and his experience here. I thought about other pilgrims who have ventured here to receive a blessing from the sea. I thought of my own pilgrimage as I've grown in my faith. I listened to the waves coming into shore with their swish . . . swish . . . swish. And I could almost hear the long, sought-after blessing of the sea, the Master of the sea echoed in each wave: *I . . . love . . . you. I . . . love . . . you. I . . . love . . . you.*

Now I see. Now I *sea*. Now I see.

Faith, hope, and love. But the greatest of these is love.

For where your treasure is,
there your heart will be also.

—Luke 12:34, NIV

Chapter 22

TREASURE CHEST

Photographic Memories

I adore taking pictures. From my early days as a third grader on the Norfolk Harbor Tour, taking pictures of little more than the railing in my line of vision, I have been a shutterbug. I'll never forget how my family roared with laughter when we got *that* roll of film developed. "Nice railing, Jen!" "Oooh, here's a beaut of the mesh screen *beneath* the railing!" Don't worry; I wasn't scarred for life or anything. I persevered through my early photographic failures.

I keep a camera with me most of the time. I just like capturing special places, special moments, and special people. It's like "freezing time." Happy memories make life rich. If my house were on fire, the only material thing I would risk saving would be my pictures. I also love receiving pictures from family and friends of good times shared. I have a dear friend from childhood named Karen. We grew up together in Norfolk, but we haven't seen each other in years. We live in different states and have mutually busy lives raising families. We may not talk often, but the bond between us will never be severed and can never be diminished. Besides, as Christians we know we'll have eternity to gab and be as goofy as we were as teenagers.

Karen's family is also very dear to me. From time to time, her father sends pictures of Karen and me as teenagers with a brief note of fond remembrance. He gives me gifts of "frozen time" from my childhood. There we were, sitting on a sand dune at Jockey's Ridge, North Carolina, with our matching Farrah Fawcett hairdos (scary). And there we were at the beach, smiling as if we thought every cute surfer boy would no doubt want to meet us (ignorance is bliss). Looking at those pictures I sat for the longest time, reliving those moments and "thawing" those tidbits of time with the warmth in my heart.

I could see us driving Karen's old car to the beach, windows rolled down, listening to our favorite Eagles or Steve Miller tune. ("Oh, don't you just *love* that song?!) I could smell the Coppertone suntan lotion we'd put on as we asked each other, "Does this suit make me look fat?" I could hear our giggles, our silly stories, and our daily synopsis of all the cute boys on the beach. In my head, I can still hear these words: "Oh, he is SO CUTE! I saw him put his surfboard on top of his car! His license plate is JAX146! I've just GOT to meet him!" (Karen is now red in the face with embarrassment as she reads this. The very fact that I remember that plate number after 20 years is a good indicator of how many times she said it.)

Ah, memories. What a gift! Ah, *friends*. What an even greater gift! Have you ever just stopped and thought about all the friends you've had and loved throughout your life? It takes my breath away to consider how richly I've been blessed with special people. What a privilege to have friends. I don't think I have ever just stopped and thanked God collectively for the friends He has brought into my life.

My friends have shaped me, taught me, changed me, encouraged me, and yes, sometimes hurt me. My friends have given me laughter, unbridled fun, wisdom, knowledge, humility, grace, forgiveness, gifts, tears, and precious memories. What could be greater treasure? Howard Hughes, the billionaire, once said, "I'd give it all for one good friend."[1] The richest man in the world had an empty treasure chest. His bank vault was full, but his heart was empty. True treasure doesn't have a monetary value. Just as pirates of old used to bury their treasure for safekeeping, we too should protect our treasure in the chest of our hearts.

> "A man of many companions may come to ruin, but there is a friend who sticks closer than a brother" (Proverbs 18:24, ESV).

It really is a small world. I have been dumbfounded by the people I have met across my life who are somehow connected to someone else I know. Did you hear about the "Six Degrees from Kevin Bacon" game that was going around Hollywood a few years back? People would stand around at parties and figure out how they were connected to the actor Kevin Bacon by the chain of people they knew. It was silly, but what a point it makes. We have numerous acquaintances and companions throughout life, people we know and would consider "casual friends." It's nice to have people to know in different phases of life, but ones that you don't necessarily allow deep into your soul. Some might get deeper than others, but never reach the status of a close friend.

True friendship cannot materialize unless that inner chamber of your heart is opened for entry. We cannot handle a crowd in that chamber; we can only emotionally deal with a small number of people in our hearts at that level. Like the verse above says, someone who tries to have too many friends may come to ruin. It is foolhardy to try to open yourself up to more than you can handle. Not just from a vulnerability standpoint, but from the sheer emotional outlay required. I think we throw around the term "friend" much too loosely.

I love the second half of that verse: "but there is a friend who sticks closer than a brother." What a beautiful verse! What a picture of loyalty, perseverance, commitment, and love. It is these "sticky friends" whom I will be talking about for the rest of this chapter.

Reasons, Seasons, or Life

> People come into your life for a reason, a season, or a lifetime. When you figure out which it is, you'll know exactly what to do.
> —*Michelle Ventor*[2]

What does this great quote say to you? What this quote says to me is that you'll know how to appreciate the why's of a friend encounter, the when's of a friend encounter, and the permanence of a friend encounter. You'll know how long to hold on . . . and when to let go. You'll understand the commitment required to maintain and nurture those friendships. But I think reason and season friends can become lifetime friends as well.

Friends who have come into my life for a reason are easy to identify. Some have come to teach me something I needed to learn and to help me grow. Others have come as encouragers when I was in a down phase of life. I needed an emotional jump start, and there they were. Others have come as pure fun dispensers, just great pals to hang out with for hours on end. I've also had friends come into my life as an answer to prayer.

When I moved from Virginia to Georgia as a teenager, I had to tell Karen and my other friends goodbye. My heart was broken to leave the coast and those I loved with all my heart. Then one day at my new school, another Karen walked into my homeroom class, and I was immediately drawn to her. She had the same bad attitude I had; she had also just moved inland from the coast and didn't like it one bit either. We became fast friends and remain close to this day. I didn't substitute one Karen for another; I was blessed to have a new friend in my life to fill the hole in my heart, and to be with me in a new season of maturity. God then brought a whole new group of companions into my life to make it full.

I've had some friends come into my life for a season, and then move on. I'm sure you have, too. There are people you befriend during certain life phases that you don't hold onto for the long haul. It may be during childhood, certain years of school or college, when you are involved in a church or other organization for a time, or at a particular job. Think of someone God brought into your life for a season, and just remember that friendship for a moment.

Me and Jenny were just like peas and carrots. —*Forrest Gump*[3]

I've always enjoyed having guy friends. Maybe it's the tomboy in me that just likes hanging around guys. For our annual weeklong family reunions, I was the only girl out of ten cousins. I had to keep up with those nine boys in flashlight freeze-tag, Sliding Rock, croquet, and putt-putt golf. So, I guess I got my basic training there. But it goes deeper somehow. I have such a healthy, close relationship with my father that I just easily relate to guys. I thoroughly enjoy talking with them because I am a straight shooter, and guys don't seem to get caught up in the communication games like gals do. Of course, I love my gal pals, and adore talking, shopping, buying clothes, and all the other girly habits that the female gender enjoys. But I am thankful for the guy friends I've made across the years. I think we learn much from having friends in both camps. Jesus certainly had both guys and gals in His circle of friends, and they ministered to Him and were blessed by Him.

I had one special guy friend for a season. Kim was a coworker of mine, and we had a great working relationship. We became solid friends and would have lengthy philosophical discussions about life. Kim was on quite a spiritual journey and would ask me questions without end. He often said I was the only friend he could talk to about such things. Perhaps I was brought into Kim's life for a reason, but he was in mine for a short season. He was tragically killed, and I will never totally get over that loss. But Kim and I will have eternity to cut up and talk at length about things. Never take friends for granted—they may be yours only for a brief season.

> "Wounds from a friend can be trusted, but an enemy multiplies kisses" (Proverbs 27:6, NIV).

Have you ever been hurt by a friend? I have. Sometimes it's hard to understand how someone so close and dear to your heart could inflict pain. But it happens. From what I can gather, unless it is you yourself who does something wrong, it is usually something that changes within the heart of that friend that causes the hurt. Sometimes those friendships can't survive, and the season of that relationship is over. But for those friendships that do survive, it is an incredible testament to the depth of your relationship.

One of the most important elements of any relationship is trust. If a friend can trust you enough to be honest with you—even when it hurts—you have a treasure in that friend. If the trust doesn't run deep, that friendship will remain shallow. Enemies multiply kisses, but true friends will shoot straight with you.

> "A friend loves at all times" (Proverbs 17:17, NIV).

Have you ever hurt a friend? Ouch, I have. I would never intentionally do so, but sometimes my imperfect, selfish actions inflict pain. Nothing makes my stomach sink faster than hurting someone I love. I immediately want the forgiveness and grace of that friend, and a true friend will deliver. A true friend loves at all times, and a true friend trusts even the wounds you inflict. If you have such a treasure of a friend, but there is a wound that needs to be healed, for heaven's sake, fix it. Hang on to that friendship; it is too precious to lose. We all need friends who will love us when we are unlovable.

Friendship is a single soul dwelling in two bodies. —*Aristotle*

Do you know what I love about God? He never stops bringing people into our lives to make our treasure chests full with the treasure of friendship. I have lifetime friends I've known for decades. But I also have lifetime friends I've only known for a couple of years. These dear friends broaden my horizons with every joke, every tear, every discussion, every adventure, and every encounter. It is a treasure for me to support my friends when they need me, and to be supported in kind when I need them.

"I thank my God every time I remember you" (Philippians 1:3, NIV).

Let me encourage you to occasionally tell your friends what they mean to you.

Thank you, my friend. Thank you, my one heart, for all you've done for me, and meant to me. Thank you for continuing to love me when I let you down. Thank you for buoying me when I feel like I'm going to sink. Thank you for the privilege of supporting you. Thank you for the sheer fun and joy you've given me; for the bike rides, taco omelets, beach walks, and emails . . . for the hugs, the coffee, the conversation, the political debates, and the prayers. Thank you for the music, movies, books, and meals we've shared. Thank you for just listening when I needed to do all the talking. Thank you for keeping my photo albums full. And thank you for the honor of being counted as a friend in the inner chamber of your heart.

"Greater love hath no man than this, that a man lay down his life for his friends" (John 15:13, KJV).

What a Friend We Have in Jesus—I love that hymn. How often do we really think about Jesus as a friend? The Creator of the universe, the Controller of the cosmos . . . wants to be your lifetime friend. He doesn't want to come into your life for just a reason or a season, but for a lifetime.

Would you die for a friend? That's a toughie. Jesus did. He laid down his life to save you, His friend. Try to imagine what kind of love that must be. My little mind can't take it in. The God of the universe and of all time considered me a good enough friend to die for. He valued me as treasure enough to preserve and protect.

> "I no longer call you servants, because a servant does not know his master's business. Instead, I have called you friends, for everything I have learned from my Father I have made known to you" (John 15:15, NIV).

Not only did He die for you, but Jesus also shared with you all He learned from His Father. Talk about the inside scoop! His dad is GOD, and He's told you all He's learned from Him. My little mind *really* can't grasp that type of friendship.

Jesus is the best friend you could ever have! He loves you no matter what. He trusts you even when you hurt Him. But He will *never* hurt you. He is there 24/7, all the time, any hour of the day. He's never too busy for you. No, you can't sit down and talk face-to-face (at least not until Heaven). But you can do something even better—you can sit down and talk heart-to-heart.

Jesus has a way of penetrating our souls more deeply than any human friend ever could. Because no matter how much we allow a friend into the chamber of our heart, we always stop just short of the throne in the chamber. We always hold back something. Perhaps it's the fear of having someone know all there is to know. There's always some dark corner we don't want people to see. But Jesus—oh, Jesus—there's no need to hold back. Not only does He know us better than we know ourselves, including what's in that dark corner, He is the only one who is worthy to sit on the throne of our hearts. And somehow deep inside, we know it, too.

Jesus is the perfect heart-chamber guest. He only comes in when He is invited and welcomed. He doesn't force His way into our chamber because friendship with Jesus is a choice. What a friend we have in Jesus. What a friend, indeed.

If you and Jesus haven't met, much less become friends, you're missing out on *the* friendship of a lifetime. He is there for every reason and every season. He stands ready to enter your heart, but He respectfully waits to be invited in.

"So, matey. How's ye treasure chest? Be it full? No? I jest shared the secret ta where X marks the spot—in ye heart." (Sorry, I just had to try some pirate-speak. I think it was as good as my railing photos.)

See, the former things have taken place, and new things I declare;
before they spring into being I announce them to you.
—Isaiah 42:9, NIV

Chapter 23

MOONDANCE

I have been given the most precious gift. This gift wasn't bought; it is priceless. This gift wasn't wrapped; it can't be contained. This gift is perhaps the most perfect gift that anyone could ever give me. But this gift has one drawback—it won't remain the same as time goes on. It will change and perhaps even become smaller for a time before it grows again. It will also get to a point where part of it will branch off and be given to someone else.

Even though these changes won't occur for quite some time, my heart breaks to think of the gift not staying the same forever. But I know deep down inside that I really *want* the gift to change and grow and move on because that is how it should be. Not to share the gift would kill it. Therein lies the mystery and the condition for holding this tremendous gift.

This is the gift: my red-haired, blue-eyed, freckle-faced six-year-old little boy is totally and unashamedly in love with me. Alex radiates extreme love and joy that brightens my heart with every word, laugh, or expression he makes. He loves to snuggle down and hold hands. He loves to tell me that I am "beautiful as a rainbow" and that he wishes I could marry two people so he could marry me someday. And . . . he loves to dance.

Alex and I have "dates" at the lake house dock on warm summer nights. Early in the day Alex will whisper in my ear, "Hey mommy, let's have a date tonight." He hasn't been turned down yet. A requirement is that no one else is around. We swing in the hammock and put on a favorite CD. Then I wait until I hear those three sweet words, "Mommy, let's dance!" We twirl and spin all over that dock. And it's our little secret.

We've had a wonderful summer of dates and dancing, but it is time for the seasons to change. Fall is here, and although I love the colors and the happy events associated with this season, I always have a hard time letting summer go. Summer is my favorite season.

Although the calendar says October, the weather still says it's summer. I just had to squeeze in one last summer hurrah, so Alex and I buzzed down to the beach at St. George Island for a long weekend. It was a wonderful weekend of fun in the sun . . . and fun under the moon. We got to the island at nighttime. After unloading the car, we grabbed our flashlights and walked down to the beach. I *love* the beach at night. The sand is cool to the toes, and the breeze is inviting to the spirit. The moon glistens on the water, lighting up the cresting waves. Fishing boats dot the horizon with red and green lights. The sound of the waves crashing on the shore seems louder than in the daytime. And the stars! Oh, how they light up the sky. They feel close enough to touch.

One of our favorite things to do is to chase ghost crabs with our flashlights. These crabs litter the waterline, with hundreds of them darting across the sand into the water. Occasionally we'll encounter "defiant" crabs that hold up their claws in protest to our intrusion, saying, "Hey! Enough with the light already!"

Nighttime at the beach. It is cool, magical, and romantic. And this—*this* is a night to remember. As Alex and I walk along the beach, we see not one but two shooting stars. God's fireworks. We find some "rare" shells glistening in the moonlight, which are definite keepers. We stroll along the water's edge and wade a little too deep, getting our shorts wet. Ah, but who cares? We stand in one place holding hands while the water comes and goes, covering our feet with wet sand. It's a race to see who "loses" his feet first. And then I hear those three sweet words, "Mommy, let's dance!" So, under the shooting stars and to the sound of the surf, Alex and I have our moondance, beneath the cover of October skies.

Just as the tides and the seasons change, so too does life change. I soak up these treasured times with Alex, for I know that our relationship will someday also change. Oh, he'll never stop loving me, but he will get to the point where he'll have other date prospects in mind. And I'm sure there will be a twinge of sadness and jealousy in my heart when that happens. But there will also be warmth in my heart to see Alex grow into a fine, loving man, as he should.

Why do we resist change? We get settled in our ways and comfortable with the way things are. Sometimes we don't welcome change even when it's for our own good. It takes too much emotional effort. If we could only embrace change with open arms, I think life would be much easier. If you're like me, though, you fight the change . . . every step of the way.

But there is a time for change.

> There is a time for everything, and a season for every activity under the heavens: a time to be born and a time to die, a time to plant and a time to uproot, a time to kill and a time to heal, a time to tear down and a time to build, a time to weep and a time to laugh, a time to mourn and *a time to dance* . . . (Ecclesiastes 3:1–4, NIV, emphasis mine)

As I look at Alex, I know the changes headed his way. I know how he will change physically, mentally, emotionally, and spiritually. But Alex doesn't. He's just content with living life day-to-day, oblivious to the coming change.

Isn't it the same with God and us? God looks at us, knowing the changes headed our way. But He knows more as a parent than we do. He knows about coming changes in relationships, changes in jobs, changes in financial status, and changes in family structure. On a larger scale He knows about changes in world events, changes in the environment, and changes in cultural make-up. He knows about these changes long before they happen.

If He knows the changes that are going to affect your life long before they happen, don't you think He is well prepared to help you cope with the change? Of course He is. Even though we act "defiant" and hold up our fists, saying, "Hey! Enough with the change already!" God remains the steady, knowledgeable Father to guide us through change.

Do you know why change is so hard? We become vulnerable for a time, and we don't like that feeling. It's what I like to call the "lobster law of change." Brent Mitchell gives a great analogy about lobsters and how we're not much different when it comes to change. He explains that lobsters are protected with strong, spiny shells, but as they grow, they have to leave their shells behind. If they do not abandon their old shells, they become trapped unto themselves and die.

Mitchell says that "the tricky part for the lobster is the brief period of time between when the old shell is discarded and the new one is formed. During that terribly vulnerable period, the transition must be scary to the lobster. Currents gleefully cartwheel them from coral to kelp. Hungry schools of fish are ready to make them a part of their food chain. For a while at least, that old shell must look pretty good."[1] I'm sure that lobster has thoughts of squeezing back into its old shell where it's protected and where it can hide. But that's not only unrealistic; it's dangerous.

Don't we sometimes have those same lobsterish thoughts? When change becomes too difficult or too scary, don't we wish we could run back to our old shells? To our "good ol' days?" To our old ways? To our old selves? But, just as with the lobster, going back is not only unrealistic, it's dangerous. It's dangerous because if we don't grow and adapt to new shells, we'll die in a prison of stagnancy. I don't mean physically; I mean emotionally, mentally, and spiritually. Plus, it's unnatural.

What if I wanted Alex to act the same way with me when he's 30, having loving eyes for no one else but me? That would be unnatural and unhealthy. He would miss the joy that he was meant to know in finding the love and soulmate of his life.

Change is hard, but it is necessary for growth. If you can embrace change in that light, it will become a blessed event for your spirit. Once the time of vulnerability is passed, you will be free to grow and expand your horizons. So, try and embrace change . . . even when it hurts.

I embrace the coming change for Alex for his sake. But for now, I'll look forward to hearing those three sweet words and having moondances. Alex is my dance partner for a season, but I will be able to revel in this precious gift for a lifetime. For when the moondance is no longer in my feet, it will ever be in my heart.

Your path led through the sea,
your way through the mighty waters,
though your footprints were not seen.
—Psalm 77:19, NIV

Chapter 24

VANISHING FOOTPRINTS

I love to racewalk, especially to great music. I can be seen doing that duck-waddling fast pace down by the river while playing air guitar or drums to my favorite tunes. I'm sure it provides great amusement for people driving by. I don't care, though. I'm in my own world, doing my thing, and loving every minute of it.

When I walk on the beach, however, the only tune I need to hear is that of the surf. I leave my earbuds at home and walk to the rhythm of the waves that seek to grab my feet as I walk past on the wet sand. Early morning beach walks are my favorite. What an incredible way to start the day, especially when a pod of dolphin cruises along with me. But they are the only company I welcome. I like the beach all to myself and don't like to have someone back there following me. Well, OK, if it's a funny sandpiper, he can race-tiptoe behind me. And when my walk is through, I love to jump into the water and cool off. Ahhhhhhhh.

I like to keep my sneakers on while I racewalk the beach. I shed them of course for the remainder of the day to keep my feet happily playing in the sand. To get a solid footing, you must walk where the sand has gotten just wet enough to become hard. If it's too wet, you sink. If it's too dry, you get stuck, and it slows your pace. The trick is to pay close attention to the movement of the water and adjust your path to the waves' good pleasure. I amuse people at the beach as well, walking fast while dodging the waves near my feet. I've seen plenty of beach chair quarterback smiles as proof of that.

On a recent walk I was struck by an amazing analogy. It is impossible to walk on the beach without leaving footprints. Try it. You won't be able to keep from giving clues that you were there. If someone is following you, they can find you. But if your walk is close enough to the water, on firm, wet sand, the footprints vanish with the enveloping nature of the beach-landing waves. Not a trace remains that you were there. What a beautiful picture of sin and grace.

It is impossible to walk through life without sinning. Try it. You won't be able to keep from giving clues that you were there. But if your walk is close enough to Christ, the enveloping nature of His grace washes that sin away. Not a trace remains that you were there, at least not in a sinful way in God's eyes. The death that seeks to follow your sin and capture you can't find you. You are free from that stalker. I think it's visually amusing to consider. Death says, "Hey, where'd that sinful guy go?" To which God replies, "His sin has been swallowed up by the waves of My grace, and you'll never find him." The next thing to be swallowed is the pesky stalker himself.

> "Death has been swallowed up in victory" (1 Corinthians 15:54, NIV).

How liberating! How exhilarating! What a rush! God is not only so good, but He is also just plain cool. He made us to come walk His beach, breathe the salt air, feel the wind blow our hair, play in His sand, dodge the waves, and enjoy the beauty of all He has to offer. He desires us to walk within the reach of His grace but loves us so much that He leaves that choice to us.

Hug that waterline while you're walking and don't get too far in dry sand where you'll get stuck. And after you've walked awhile, lose the sneakers. Jump in and let those waves cover you with their cool, refreshing, healing saltiness. Let the water wash away your exertion and your sweat. Give it all up to the sea, and to the Wavemaker Himself. You'll never feel better.

PART FIVE

NOW I SEA EVEN MORE

There is a tide in the affairs of men,
Which taken at the flood, leads on to fortune.
Omitted, all the voyage of their life is bound
in shallows and in miseries.
On such a full sea are we now afloat.
And we must take the current when it serves or lose our ventures.
—William Shakespeare

Remember your word to your servant,
for you have given me hope.
—Psalm 119:49, NIV

Chapter 25

THE NAUTILUS SHELL

I stood on the beach in such despair. No one else was around, and I let the tears flow freely.

"Oh, God! Please help me! I need some hope. I don't know if we're going to make it. Everything looks so bleak. This storm is too strong for me. I just don't know how long I can go on like this. But I don't know what else to do. Please, please, God! Forgive me for asking, but can you give me some sort of sign that we're going to make it? Can you help me find a perfect nautilus shell to help me know if we will get through this?"

Before this brisk March day, I had been looking for nautilus shells, my favorite kind to collect. I call them nautilus shells but technically they aren't, I guess. The shells I love have spirals that curve around in motion with color and beauty. Some are moon shells, some are broken whelk shells; some I don't even know their identity. Some are smooth, and some have bumpy edges. But they all swirl in the same way, and so have become categorized as nautilus shells in my mind's eye. How strange. I usually find a couple of these gems on each walk. But I had walked for two days and had yet to find one. At the end of this second day, I still didn't find one, even after my request. My heart sank. "Does this mean, 'No'?" The sun set on my hope.

But then came the third day.

I spoke to a group of women at a church on the Island. Following my talk, they gave me a nice gift certificate as a thank-you. Then the lady turned to me and said, "We'd also like to give you this."

It was an enormous, perfect nautilus shell.

Tears rushed to my eyes, but these were tears of joy from hope restored. God whispered in my ear, *"When you asked Me for a sign in the form of a nautilus shell, you had in mind something small. Oh, My little one! How I want to give you more hope than you could ever imagine! I didn't want to give you a small shell found on a beach as an answer, but a huge, affirmative 'YES!' shell coming from an unexpected place. For YES, you not only are going to make it, but you will make it in unexpected ways. Trust Me and hang on tight to Me—even when things don't appear as if this promise will hold true."*

I brought the perfect nautilus shell home, and I looked at it every day. One day I was reading my Bible and came across this verse: "Remember your word to your servant, for you have given me hope. My comfort in my suffering is this: Your promise preserves my life" (Psalm 119:49–50, NIV). Out in the margin by this verse I wrote, "The Nautilus Shell." This verse would become an anchor that I would cling to in the days ahead.

For the days did indeed get darker; darker than I ever conceived they could be. Never had my heart known such pain. Never had my hope been so destroyed. Never had my tears flowed so profusely. Many times, I thought, "Well, this is it. It's over. There's no way we could get past this. It's impossible."

And then I would remember the promise. And I would remember the nautilus shell. And I would hold on for another day. *"Remember, little one. Trust Me and hang on tight to Me—even when things don't appear as if this promise will hold true."*

Many 11th hour miracles occurred. Sometimes they came and I thought the worst was behind us. Yet another squall would come, sometimes fiercer than the one before. I almost drowned in my despair. So, I would quote it again and again: *Remember your word to your servant, for you have given me hope.*

Finally, a day came when I knew the storm was blowing itself out. Miracles began to occur with greater frequency, and now they weren't countered by squalls. It was if God had finally said to the storm, *"Hush, be still. Leave My little one alone. She's had enough."*

I was able to see the sun for the first time in a long while. It shone on my face and dried my tears each time they fell. And they fell less and less. It was time to go back to the beach. It was time for salvage after the storm. And it was time for God to whisper again to me—for me to hear His words of comfort at this sacred place of sand and sea.

I went alone. I rested and prayed. I prayed and I read. I cried and wrote. But most of all . . . I listened. I wanted answers. I had longed to find someone who could relate to my pain—someone who could identify with all I had been through. Some would come close, but never close enough to truly identify with my pain and my heart. I had resolved to give up that quest.

But then came the third day.

I said, "Lord, you came here and lived on earth, but you didn't really experience the specific things I did. Yes, you were betrayed, but in a different way. You indeed suffered more than I ever will, but still . . . I guess you can sympathize with my pain but not totally relate to it."

He spoke to me and said, *"Oh, but I* did *experience the specific things you did. I felt them on the cross 2,000 years before they happened. I know EXACTLY how you feel because I felt it first. Remember, I not only took your sins upon Myself, but I took on your sorrows as well. I took on the things others have done to you. So, My little one, I know exactly how you feel, and I share your pain in every tiny detail."*

My heart burst with relief, joy, and the realization that I was not alone—and never had been. Jesus could relate to my pain because He had felt it fully . . . and *first.* In truth, He felt it more because He *paid* for it. It doesn't matter what we go through. He's already been there, done that. I will never be alone in my pain. Somehow, I forgot this when the days were dark and the storm was raging, and God seemed so far away. I had to be reminded. *"Remember, little one. Trust Me and hang on tight to Me—even when things don't appear as though this promise will hold true."*

Once again, I was standing on the beach. And once again, I asked for a nautilus shell. "God," I said, "you've already given me more than I ever could have imagined or wanted. You've kept your promise. We *are* going to make it. And I'm grateful beyond words. So, I don't really need this, but it would be a nice remembrance of this time here with you to find a perfect nautilus shell to take home."

I looked down and didn't see a perfect nautilus shell. I saw two broken pieces of a nautilus shell, in the perfect shapes of a "J" and a "C" lying side by side. I picked them up and studied them in my hand. Another verse came to mind: "This is my body, which is broken for you"

(1 Corinthians 11:24, KJV). Jesus Christ had walked in my shoes 2,000 years before I even knew how to walk. He had come to take on my sins . . . and my sorrows. He had come to provide a way out of the storm and into peace, both eternally and within the confines of time on Earth. So, when the day came when I cried, "Oh, God! Please help me. I need some hope," He was able to respond, "*Oh My little one! How I want to give you more hope than you could ever imagine!*"

A broken J and C from a nautilus shell. Nothing could be more hopeful. Nothing could be more affirming. And nothing could be more perfect:

> **J**esus **C**hrist: a Savior broken, but through brokenness came hope.
> **J**enny **C**ote: a woman broken, but through brokenness came growth.
> **J**enny and **C**asey: two people broken, but through brokenness came renewal.

I sat again at home and looked at my nautilus shells. The broken pieces are lovingly displayed in a shadowbox frame so I will never forget the true promise of hope for all the storms I face. I gave thanks to God for having given me that anchor of hope as I entered into the stormiest days of my life. I gave thanks for the words He whispered in my heart and for the words He led me to in Scripture. "Remember" was our common word together.

I studied the large, "perfect" nautilus shell and I began to ask myself, "Why is it that I love these particular shells so much? Sure, they are beautiful, but so are many other types of shells. Why am I so drawn to the nautilus?" Then it hit me. The nautilus shell is a picture of a storm. The swirling spiral looks just like a hurricane. And there in the middle is the eye. The calm eye in the middle of the storm. The nautilus shell for me is a picture of life, with the hope of God holding me tight in the center. No wonder I love them so.

And yes, we did make it . . . because long ago there was a third day.

Amazing grace! (how sweet the sound)
That sav'd a wretch like me!
I once was lost, but now am found,
Was blind, but now I see.

—John Newton, Amazing Grace[1]

Chapter 26

I ONCE WAS BLIND, BUT . . .

As a wordsmith, I like words and phrases that make the reader sit up and take notice. Some tools in the author's arsenal are intentionally misspelled words or ill-matched phrases that make the reader do a double take, either because they don't make sense or because distorting the proper phrase triggers mental dissonance. "Keep your eyes wide shut." See?

Often, however, such phrases trigger mental dissonance because we can identify with them all too well. How many times have you been absolutely blind to what you were doing or to what was going on around you because the truth you didn't want to see was "hiding in plain sight?" (See?) You just didn't see it, or you just didn't *want* to see it. Physical blindness isn't a choice, but many times mental, emotional, or spiritual blindness is.

The title of the book you hold in your hands was born on April 5, 2000, at 4:40 p.m. I was walking up from the beach and noticed that the beach house next to ours on St. George Island, Florida, had been renamed. I stood in the middle of the road, clad only in flip-flops and a bathing suit, and stared at the new sign for a moment. A thought then suddenly came to me: *That would make a great title for a book.* The name of the house was Now I Sea. (Misspelled word.)

I walked on to our beach house, asked to borrow a legal pad from my friend Gena, and went back down to the beach where I penned the prologue. Words tumbled out of my heart and mind onto the yellow college-ruled pages that over the next few hours became smeared with suntan lotion and sand. I can't explain the exhilaration of that afternoon. I didn't realize it then, but I was born an author that day. That one sign with a cleverly misspelled word had grabbed my attention so much that it inspired not only one book, but now a dozen of them, and started an entirely new tack in my vocational life course.

At the time, I was working in marketing, strategic planning, and business development at Scottish Rite Children's Medical Center in Atlanta, Georgia. While it was rewarding to help sick kids, I had a "divine discontent" that I was not doing what God had wired me to do or what He had put me on this planet to do. But as I sat there staring out to sea, the sea breeze gently lifting the pages of the legal pad, and the ink filling the Hawaiian Tropic-smudged paper, I could almost hear God whisper in my ear, *This is what you were born to do, and this is how I will use you to bless My world.*

I returned home to Atlanta and began to write. I wrote chapters as they came to me, or as I traveled to salty destinations. (You can see the log of when and where I wrote each chapter in the Notes and Sources section.) I would stay up late and work on the weekends, obsessed with this new adventure. Work had never been so fun or exciting. In fact, although it required work, it didn't *feel* like work. That is a clue to know you are doing what you were meant to do in life. When you are living out your purpose with passion, the required long hours mean nothing, and your work is not drudgery, but joy! Although I knew research, writing, and marketing very well, I knew nothing about publishing books. And as I still had a day job, I didn't have time to pursue traditional publishing, so I decided to simply self-publish the book. Learning all of that professional author-y stuff would come later.

> "Do not despise these small beginnings, for the Lord rejoices to see the work begin . . ." (Zechariah 4:10, NLT).

I must confess to you that at the outset of this endeavor my motives were not entirely pure. Blame it on my sinful nature or on my wiring as a marketer, but thoughts sailed through my mind, such as, *Maybe I can be a famous Christian author like Max Lucado! Maybe I can make a lot of money writing!* Ah, the shallow fantasies we silly humans entertain. I was utterly blind to what I was thinking. But God was not.

Just as *Now I Sea* rolled off the press, a Category 5 life storm hit me. My husband's struggle with addiction had been building like a tropical depression out in the ocean, looming nearer and nearer to the coast of our lives as it gained strength. When it finally made landfall, this devastating life storm gutted me, leaving debris in its wake. But my foundation remained solid, for it had been built not on the sand, but on the Rock of Christ. Of course, Satan was out to destroy my husband, to destroy me, and to destroy our family, but he was also out to keep me from ever becoming God's scribe.

> "And we know that in all things God works for the good of those who love him, who have been called according to his purpose" (Romans 8:28, NIV).

But Satan was the blind one now, for in reality God had used *him* to do His bidding. For it was through this storm that God saved Casey, our marriage, and our family, all the while putting me through His Holy boot camp. I wasn't fit to be His scribe until the other side of this life storm. Beware of the occupational hazard of working for God. If He is your Boss, anything you say, think, write, or do will be put to the test. I had to live out and prove everything I had written in *Now I Sea* to be true as I weathered this storm. God faithfully kept His promises and deluged us with His amazing grace. Casey healed, I healed, and our family healed with time.

Initially I hesitated to share my life storm as it first blew onshore. My pathetic thoughts went something like this: *What will people think if a Christian author like me has a broken family from addiction?* I was terrified that my *Now I Sea* readers would become disillusioned and deflated if they knew that such life storms were real, and that I wasn't a paragon of virtue. As *if.*

My eyes were wide shut. I was completely blind as to what was happening. I was being played like a fiddle by the deceiver with the oldest trick in the book: pride.

If Satan can keep you quiet and have you hide behind a false façade, he not only keeps you in his delightful prison of torment, but he prevents you from ministering to others. But once you speak TRUTH, it immediately takes the wind out of his black sails. His methods lose all power to manipulate you and keep you locked away from peace, comfort, and healing. When Jesus commanded the storm on Galilee to "HUSH!", it instantly blew itself out. And that is exactly what Jesus did for me. But then He instructed me, *"Jenny, if you want to write for Me, it's got to be 100 percent about me, and 0 percent about you. Got it?"* Immediately, something like scales of shame fell from my eyes, and I could see. Clearly.

I became completely transparent about my story, as did Casey. As we shared what we had endured, people came out of the woodwork whispering, "You, too? Can you help us through our storm?" Liberation is a beautiful thing! This salvage after the storm enriched our spiritual walk, strengthened our marriage and family, allowed us to minister to others, and deepened my pen.

My writing dreams were put on hold for two years until the cleanup was complete, and I was emptied of myself and my personal ambitions of being an author. I told my Boss, "I couldn't care less about fame or money. I just want to use my pen for Your glory!"

That's when God caused a little Scottish terrier and a little black cat living in our home to inspire a book about the animals heading to Noah's Ark. I stood on the precipice of a new voyage into the literary world with a traditional publisher, and it was my husband Casey who made it possible for me to set sail full time into the writing world with the release of *The Ark, the Reed, and the Fire Cloud.* Since 2008, God has used my pen to reach kids around the globe with HIStory, and it has been the most blessed adventure of a lifetime.

But *Now I Sea* sat there on Amazon, all alone and adrift as my authoring attention shifted to my new genre of historical fiction books. It's not that I didn't love this book, but my focus was now immersed in another literary sea. Until one day in 2023 when I had a request from Pastor Jack Hibbs at Calvary Chapel Chino Hills, California, to reprint *The Longest Days* chapter for his church. And God told me to revisit this first writing assignment and get it shipshape just for you. It has been an utter joy to mend the sails, add new rigging, repaint the hull, and set a new course for

Now I Sea. But God also wanted me to write this chapter so you would know the story behind the story—behind the story.

It was a couple of years after I began writing this book before I finally met our next-door neighbors at St. George Island and asked them how they came up with the name *Now I Sea*. They shared that after a weekend spent at the beach with no name yet determined, they were driving off the island and someone in the car began humming *Amazing Grace*. And the name just naturally spilled out. I once was blind, but . . . Now I Sea.

I face-palmed. It hadn't even dawned on me that the beloved hymn would have inspired the name. How could I have been so blind?! It thrilled my heart to know the origin of the name, for the story of *Amazing Grace* was also born in a storm.

John Newton was about as vile and disgusting as a human could possibly be. He was a foul-mouthed slave trader who caused foul-mouthed sailors to blush and raise their eyebrows in shock from the debased vocabulary and colorful metaphors that spewed from his mouth. I imagine this wretch looking (and smelling) like one of the filthy, maniacal pirates from the *Pirates of the Caribbean* movie. They were all dead men walking, living under a curse. So was John Newton. He used women, drank like a sailor, mocked believers, and shook his fist at God. Until a storm off the coast of Ireland got his attention in March 1748.

When a shipmate was washed overboard from their ship *Greyhound*, Newton lashed himself and a fellow sailor to the ship's pump. Terrified, he held on for dear life, exclaiming, "If this will not do, then Lord have mercy upon us!" They survived the storm, but those words soon began to haunt Newton. In time, not only did Newton fall at the feet of Christ in repentance, but he left slave trading to become a priest in the little vicarage of Olney, England. Talk about a radical tack in your vocational career! The slave trader would eventually become an abolitionist and champion the cause with William Wilberforce to eradicate the evil practice of slavery from England.

> "Therefore, if any man be in Christ, he is a new creature: old things are passed away; behold, all things are become new" (2 Corinthians 5:17, KJV).

John Newton and poet-parishioner friend William Cowper wrote poems and hymns as part of their tiny parish prayer meetings. In late 1772, Newton penned the lyrics to *Amazing Grace,* using it for a New Year's service on January 1, 1773.[2] The hymn remained relatively unknown even after publication of Newton and Cowper's work in 1779, *Olney Hymns.* It wasn't truly until *Amazing Grace* reached America's shores in the early nineteenth century and was put to music (with the tune you're currently humming in your head) that the song became popular. Now, two centuries later, it is the most beloved hymn in history.

> "Do not despise these small beginnings, for the LORD rejoices to see the work begin . . ." (Zechariah 4:10, NLT).

Newton's *Amazing Grace* lyrics hearken back to the New Testament stories of the Prodigal Son and Jesus healing the blind beggar. He believed that lost sinners such as himself were "blinded by the god of this world" until "mercy came to us not only undeserved but undesired . . . our hearts endeavored to shut him out till he overcame us by the power of his grace."[3]

Newton's eyes were admittedly shut wide open. He didn't want God or His grace. Like Jonah, he blindly ran. But the Hound of Heaven caught up to that wretch John Newton on the *Greyhound* in the middle of a storm. He once was blind, but . . .

If you're spiritually blind, I know a Great Physician who specializes in curing such blindness. Allow Jesus to touch your spiritual eyes so you can live life as He intended you to see and live it. If you're blind in other areas of life, you can visit the same Practice and be healed. Don't go through life with your eyes wide shut. Open them—open them wide!

I once was blind. But I hope now you sea exactly what happened to change all that.

PART SIX

BACK IN PORT

"Give me the sunlight and the sea
And who shall take my heaven from me?"
—Alfred Noyes[1]

And I saw a new heaven and a new earth:
for the first heaven and the first earth were passed away;
and there was no more sea.

—Revelation 21:1, KJV

Chapter 27

NO MORE SEA

The first few words of Eric Clapton's song *Tears in Heaven* bring tears to my eyes. These are the words of a father whose heart is broken. These are the words of a father who tragically lost a little boy who fell to his death. These are the words of anguish caused by death. I can't listen to more than a few bars of this song before I get a lump in my throat. I share the anguish, but I cannot begin to fathom how Mr. Clapton must feel. I cannot imagine such a loss. That's a Category 5 storm if I ever saw one.

When you give it some thought, what is the worst part of death—at least for those who remain? It *has* to be the separation. The immediate inability to touch, see, talk to, or hear someone you have loved is agonizing. There is nothing you can do to change the circumstances. The helplessness that accompanies the separation just adds insult to injury.

I think there are few people who have not experienced such separation from a loved one. I have experienced it many times: a grandmother, a brother-in-law, a father-in-law, an uncle, a very dear friend—but never a child. That to me must be the hardest loss. And I think the reason is that on top of the separation and the helplessness is the loss of innocence and the loss of a future that could have been . . . and *should* have been. If only.

Perhaps it is the "if only's" that are hardest to deal with. They are a natural part of the grieving process, along with shock and anger. We can't understand the "why's," either. Especially when tragedy strikes. Especially when there is a God in Heaven who saw it coming. This is the greatest mystery with which I, and most of us, struggle. I know without a doubt that God sends angels who protect us and intervene for our safety, probably more than we ever know. But in those times when intervention is not there, how can that be explained? Well, it can't. We cannot see into the details of every situation, much less the future, nor can we understand God's thought process. This is where faith gets hard, but perhaps this is where it grows. For this I *do* know—God's heart is the first to break when a separation occurs. He has experienced more separation than you and I ever will. And His heart breaks the most because He could have made things work differently.

When God made the world, He had a choice. He could make a world filled with a bunch of robots that would automatically love Him and do what He says without question. Or He could make a world filled with free spirits who could choose to love and obey Him. Tell me, would it really be love for the Creator to withhold free will from the soul of His creation? No, it would be a programmed script. Further, would that reciprocation from His creation really be love in the first scenario? No, it would be a mechanical instinct.

This is the one thing God doesn't know how to do. God doesn't know how *not* to love. He had to go with choice number two. Love is His nature. He chose to give us the freedom to either love Him or not to love Him; to obey Him or not to obey Him. And He knew the risks involved. He could see the separation coming.

He saw the separation coming from His firstborn children, Adam and Eve. He knew that a free spirit would fall prey to the sin that would entice it to do whatever it wanted. And He knew that as the domino effect of sin occurred, He would have to remain true to His choice of allowing free will to guide His creation, even though there would be pain, even though there would be loss, even though there would be separation. Even though on top of the separation there would be the loss of innocence and the loss of a future that could have been . . . and *should* have been. If only.

But there is another part of God's nature that is as strong as His unfailing love, and that is His utter commitment to justice. He is a just God and has set a high standard that a wrong must be made right. He hates sin so much that He never gives it a free pass. It must be paid for because the damage it inflicts is too costly.

And so, God's first separation experience resulted in the separation of every free spirit-filled child born thereafter, which was everyone.

Intimacy with God was lost no sooner than it began. And the tears in Heaven and on Earth began to flow. The tears seem to result from many sources of pain and difficulty in this life, but we need to realize that they truly are a result of that loss of intimacy with God. A child lost eternally from his Father—what could be more agonizing than that?

So how do you remain true to your choice of love and to your commitment to justice, yet find a way to stop the separation and the tears? Only God could have come up with this one. The only way to do this is to eliminate the chasm with a way to cross over. Literally. So that's what He did.

Intimacy involves knowing someone inside and out. Before their fall, Adam and Eve strolled through the garden with God, talking and enjoying His presence. Since God cannot be in the presence of sin, that closeness or intimacy was lost, and man lost the ability to know God inside and out. How that must have hurt God to the core. Have you ever been in a situation where someone didn't have a clear picture of who you really are as an individual? Maybe that someone thought you were cold and unfeeling when, in fact, you are warm and tenderhearted. Maybe that someone thought you didn't care about their hurt when, in fact, you wanted to be right by their side to hold their hand and console them. Maybe that someone got the wrong impression of your true intentions either by your action or inaction. It is a terrible feeling to be misunderstood. At the core of our soul is the desire to be known honestly and openly by those we love.

So, God had a problem. His own children didn't know Him. They didn't know He was warm and tenderhearted. They didn't know He wanted nothing more than to be right by their side. They didn't know the extreme love He had for them. So, God the Father had a talk with Jesus the Son. And they decided that Jesus would be able to show them who God *really* was. In living, breathing color, His children would have an opportunity to get to know Him inside and out. This was the first step required for building the cross in order to restore intimacy.

Jesus knew He had to go to Earth, so God and Jesus each shed tears. Each knew they would be separated for a time, and each knew what was coming. I'm sure it was a solemn departure when Jesus left Heaven and came to Earth. He was born like all children are. He experienced every physical discomfort and every emotion we experience. He was an infant, a toddler, a preschooler, a boy, an adolescent, and a man. He was bound to the earthly laws of cause and effect, whether they be in a physical or in an emotional sense. He learned to live with the restraints of time and of distance. He learned to live within a culture steeped in ritual and law that kept God distant . . . and seemingly cold and unfeeling. He was able to touch, see, and hear those around him. He learned to laugh, and He learned to cry. Did He ever learn to cry! This "God with skin on" experienced tears in Heaven and on Earth.

Jesus' time on Earth passed. Thirty-three years of being here on Earth was the next step needed to build the cross. He accomplished much while here. He brought a new way of thinking about God by explaining what He was really like. He removed blinders from eyes so God could be viewed accurately as warm and tenderhearted. He shared with people how God wanted nothing more than to be right by their side through every storm. Lives were changed. Bodies were healed. Souls were set free from the emotional bondage of hurt and sin.

But a time finally came when God, as Jesus, was once again in a garden under a grove of olive trees. On bended knee, a heart breaking with the thought of what must be completed to finish the cross, Jesus begged His Father, "Please, please! Let this cup pass from me. But your will be done, not mine."

God sat in Heaven with the toughest ask ever placed before Him. What was He to do? Intervene or not? I think this was God's greatest source of pain because He had a *choice* of how to answer. When He pondered His continuing love for you and me and the requirement of justice to pay the costly tab for sin, He had His answer. He had to say "No." He had to allow Jesus to go through the ultimate separation to make the cross complete for you and for me. And that ultimate separation was to become sin while nailed to a brutal Roman cross. Because God cannot remain in the presence of sin, He had to turn His back on Jesus. It was the ultimate separation. He could have prevented it but didn't—He wanted you and me back too badly. He knew we could never afford to pay the high tab for our sin, so Jesus paid the tab instead.

I think Heaven was flooded that day. The tears splashed around the very throne of God as He wept for His lost child.

The story didn't end there, in despair. There was a purpose for the tears—a good one. There was a purpose for the cross—an end to the separation. Jesus remained separated from God and life for three days, which was the last step needed to finish the cross. On the morning of the third day, it was time to bridge the chasm. Jesus was the first one across. Just before He did so, He stood in front of a stone door that had enclosed Him in another garden, a garden tomb. I can imagine Jesus figuratively standing there before it, echoing a similar sentiment to Mr. Clapton's song that beyond the door, there would be peace and no more tears in Heaven.

The stone door was rolled away, Jesus left the borrowed tomb, and God rushed back to His side. Jesus had paid the price and made the cross that would provide the end to separation for all children of God. The tears in Heaven dried up, and a party began! The joy of finding His lost child erased all the pain. God had His boy back. And He had the chance to have you back, and to have me back.

But to this day, God remains true to His vow of free choice. His love is ever strong, as is His commitment to justice. He allows us to choose to cross over the chasm of separation or not, by accepting this incredible story as truth in our hearts and agreeing to become intimate with God. Every time a lost child of God accepts the Cross of Jesus, there is a party in Heaven! The tissues are tossed into the trash, as is the sinner's tab for the sin.

No More Sea

OK, by now you must be wondering, "What in the world does the chapter title have to do with this story? Isn't this a book about spiritual insights from the sea? I don't recall having seen anything about the sea in this chapter." You are just *so* astute.

You're right, so here is the spiritual insight from the sea. The only disciple of Jesus who was not put to death for his connection with Jesus was John. Instead—lucky him—he was exiled to the island of Patmos. John was separated from those whom he loved. He was separated from the place he loved and the life he loved. He had been separated from all those who had shared with him the incredible encounter of "God with skin on," watching them die, one by one. But this allowed him to do a lot of thinking. And a lot of dreaming. And a lot of writing.

While on Patmos, John had a vision for writing the last book of the Bible. Really deep stuff. Really scary stuff at the first sound of it. Really hard-to-understand stuff. But it was really exciting stuff. John had to write things "in code" to the people of his day. The Christian persecution was in full swing, but not really by the Romans. They were just patsies for the one who started the separation from the beginning with his great ideas of sin in the Garden of Eden. Knowing full well that God had fixed the problem by offering a solution through Jesus, Satan was scared. And he remains scared to this day because he knows we have a choice. Misery loves company, and he is afraid of being separated from as many miserable people as he can deceive. So, he has tried to break the cross over the chasm of separation from God since the day the door was opened, by intimidating those who make the choice to cross. He knows he has already lost the war, but still he fights, aiming his flaming arrows of deception at the children of God.

So, in order to help those who were first in the line of fire, John wrote *Revelation*. As a dear pastor friend of mine says, he wrote about "blessings in disguise." Because that is exactly what *Revelation* is all about.

I know this book of the Bible is cloudy in many respects, but there are a couple of verses in this book that made me sit up with alarm. I was really upset when I first read this one: "And I saw a new heaven and a new earth: for the first heaven and the first earth were passed away; and there was no more sea" (Revelation 21:1, KJV).

I must be honest. When I first read that verse, I was like, "Whoa, this *must* be a typo! No more sea?! Heaven has no sea?!! How can Heaven be Heaven without the sea? . . ." But then I read between the lines and saw what John was trying to say.

To John, an exiled person on an island, the sea represented separation from all that he loved. There is a very real phenomenon that occurs among island dwellers called "island fever." Some people become overwhelmed by the separation from the mainland and suffer tremendous emotional anguish on the confines of an island. As John looked out on the beautiful briny sea each day, he was reminded that he was alone. He couldn't appreciate the beauty of the sea because of the symbol it firmly held in his mind, or so it seems to me. And in his vision of the new Heaven and the new Earth, what he saw was no more separation. He saw no more sea. So, when Jesus comes back to take us to his New World, the chasm of separation will be gone once and for all. In John's definition, there will be no more sea. There will be intimacy with God once more.

A few verses later, John says this:

> "He will wipe every tear from their eyes. There will be no more death or mourning or crying or pain, for the old order of things has passed away" (Revelation 21:4, NIV).

So, Mr. Clapton was right: There will be no more tears in Heaven.

At the beginning of this book, I proudly told you of my ancestor, Pleickard Dietrich Sailer, who was my sailing forefather. But there is one more ancestor to tell you about before we end this cruise.

Around 1675, a ship set sail from England to Boston, Massachusetts. Nine miles from shore, the ship capsized off the shore of Cape Cod, killing all but one passenger. That lone survivor was my ancestor, Nathaniel Oaks, a 16-year-old cabin boy. Nathaniel swam to shore, and as he did so, he prayed to God. He begged Him, "If I make it to shore, I will never go to the sea again." As he swam that long, tiring distance, he would lie on his back to rest. To him, the worst part of the ordeal was the intense hunger he experienced.

Well, he made it to shore, penniless, with no possessions and with no one to turn to. For the rest of his life, Nathaniel never went near the sea again. He spent his life bypassing the sea at every opportunity, opting to travel a longer route via land to get to any given destination. He wanted no more sea.

When I first heard about Nathaniel, I appreciated his courage and was amazed at how he survived, but I was upset with his attitude. I thought, "How could I, the sailor queen, have such anti-sea sentiment in my bloodline?! It's not possible." But then I tried to see things from Nathaniel's point of view. To him, as with John, the sea represented separation from life, and from all he held dear. The sea swallowed all his worldly possessions, and it nearly cost him his life. So, I can understand the plea bargain he made with God. And I know that God understood, not that God operates with plea bargains. For some reason, this one lone cabin boy was the one He chose to save from the shipwreck. Again, why intervene with this one? Who knows? Maybe He knew that in the year 2000 a certain sailor girl would someday want to write about the heart of God as best she could. Maybe He knew you needed to hear a word from Him even through her imperfect pen. And maybe He knew that that girl couldn't get here without Nathaniel *and* Dietrich. Who knows?

But remember this one thing that is for sure: Remember what God's heart is really like, even when we do not understand His reasoning. He loved us so much that He allowed Jesus to be submersed in the sea of separation for our sake. Our Father suffered the agony of separation, so we wouldn't have to experience it firsthand . . . and so there would be no more tears in Heaven.

Now, there are some who believe that "no more sea" in Heaven literally means that there will be no sea in Heaven. Sorry, I don't buy it. Sailing on the shiny blue sea here on Earth is about as close to Heaven as my little mind can imagine. If that isn't a foretaste of blissful things to come . . . I don't know what is. Besides, I don't think God would have created the sea if He didn't love it so much; and I think Heaven is called "Heaven" because it is filled with that which God loves.

So, I'm putting in a request for my mansion in Heaven to have a dock out back. Better yet, forget the mansion—a sailboat will do just fine.

Everything in your life is a reflection of a choice you have made.
If you want a different result, make a different choice.

—Anonymous

Chapter 28

SEA FOR YOURSELF

Time to disembark. It's been a wonderful cruise. Thanks for coming along. I pray our time together at the coast has been enjoyable as well as insightful for you. I know this book was filled with stories of my experiences, but I want you to hear something loud and clear. This is your captain speaking!

This book was written just for *you* and *your* experiences. God had you in mind when He whispered thoughts in my ear to put on paper. He wants you to know Him intimately. He wants to stroll hand in hand with you along the beach. He wants to take you on the sail of your life. He wants to laugh with you, cry with you, and kiss your cheek with gentle sea breezes of His love and grace. He wants to show you things in nature, in His word, and amid your experiences, if you'll let Him. He is the Supreme Admiral of the sea of life, and He wrote the Book of Navigation. Who better to be at the helm?

Sea for yourself. The next cruise is departing any minute—don't miss it. He's ready to fill your sails. Conditions are favorable, once again.

Sea You Later . . . and Godspeed,

Jenny

NOTES AND SOURCES

Below are the log entry dates, places, notes, and reference sources. I am grateful for permission to reproduce copyright material. Although I have made every reasonable attempt to locate and contact copyright holders, there remain a few authors I was unable to locate. I would be pleased to hear from any of the sources below regarding proper crediting of the work.

Foreword written by Pastor Jack Hibbs, Calvary Chapel Chino Hills, California.

Prologue: Much to Sea (written at St. George Island, Florida, on the beach, 4/5/00, 4:40 p.m.)

PART ONE: CASTING OFF

1. Peter Hamilton, from *The Restless Wind*, reprinted in *The Call of the Sea*, (Great Britain: Exley Publications Ltd., 1999, and New York: Exley Publications LLC, 1999) p. 23.

Chapter 1: Sailboat Dreams (written at Lake Burton, 4/24/00, 2:30 p.m.)

1. Thomas Lovell Beddoes (1803–49).

Chapter 2: The Love Boat (written aboard *Agape,* 8/15/00, 8:44 p.m.)

1. William Wordsworth (1770–1850), *With Ships the Sea Was Sprinkled Far and Nigh.*

Chapter 3: Daughter of a Daughter of a Sailor (written at the river, 9/17/00, 6:27 p.m.) *(This chapter is dedicated to my Uncle Willie Oaks, who found Dietrich.)*

Chapter 4: Wait and Sea (written in the beach room, 10/18/02, 2:30 p.m.)

1. Mortimer Adler, www.quotationspage.com
2. Comte de Buffon, www.quotationspage.com
3. Encyclopedia.com, Copyright 2001, Infonautics Corporation, (http://www.encyclopedia.com/articles/03729.html)
4. Thies Matzen, "In the Kingdom of Silence," *Cruising World,* Volume 28, Number 4, (New York: Miller Sports Group, LLC), April 2002, pp. 50–53.

PART TWO: SMOOTH SAILING

1. Herman Melville, (1819–1891)

Chapter 5: Run the Gunnels (written at Huntington Beach, South Carolina, 8/13/00, 2:55 p.m.)

1. Mark Twain, (This quote is attributed to Mark Twain, but has never been substantiated.)
2. Ferdinand Magellan, Explorer
3. Andre Gide, www.quotationspage.com
4. Leo Buscaglia, *Living, Loving and Learning,* (Thorofare, NJ: Slack, Incorporated, 1982), http://www.slackbooks.com/view.asp?slack code=80222.
5. Jim Rohn, The Time to Act, Messages from the Masters, 08/09/2000, (http://www.dailyinbox.com)

Chapter 6: Stay the Course (written on a flight to Dublin, Ireland, 6/11/00, 1:00 a.m.)

Chapter 7: Lighthouse Illumination (written at Lake Burton, 7/14/00, 2:18 p.m.)

1. Rod Nichols, *Keeper's Prayer,* 1999, reprinted by permission, (http://www.geocities.com/rodnichols.geo/rod2.html)
2. Alaa K. Ashmawy, The Lighthouse of Alexandria, Copyright 1995, 1999, 2000, (http://ce.eng.usf.edu/pharos/wonders/pharos.html)
3. Lighthouse Construction Types, National Maritime Initiative, 2000, (http://www.cr.nps.gov/maritime/constype/constype.htm)
4. Lighthouse Keepers in the Nineteenth Century, National Maritime Initiative, 2000, (http://www.cr.nps.gov/maritime/keep/keep19th.htm), (excerpts from Nineteenth-Century Lights: Historic Images of American Lighthouses by Candace and Mary Louise Clifford (Alexandria, VA: Cypress Communications, 2000).
5. Ibid.

6. New Point Comfort Light, National Maritime Initiative Inventory of Historic Light Stations, 1999, (http://www.cr.nps.gov/maritime/light/newptcom.htm)

PART THREE: ROUGH SEAS AND BATTERED SHORES

1. Pam Brown, in *The Call of the Sea*, (Great Britain: Exley Publications Ltd., 1999 and New York: Exley Publications LLC, 1999, p. 45.

Chapter 8: Even the Wind and the Waves (written at St. George Island, 10/6/00, 6:00 p.m.)

1. *The Disciple's Study Bible*, NIV, commentary on p. 1279. (Nashville: Holman Bible Publishers, Copyright 1988). (I would highly recommend this Bible to anyone seeking to read excellent commentary that clearly explains the Bible verse by verse.)

Chapter 9: The Red Sea (written at the river, 2/16/01, 5:16 p.m.)

Chapter 10: The Dead Sea (written at home, 2/1/01, 12:34 p.m.)

1. Jay Stuller, *Alcatraz the Prison, Essay by Jay Stuller*, (Salt Lake City: Precision Litho, copyright by Golden Gate National Parks Association, 1998) p. 2.
2. Ibid., p. 20.
3. Ibid., back cover.

Chapter 11: The Longest Days (written in the beach room, July 28, 2001, 12:27 p.m.)

1. From D-DAY: "June 6, 1944—The Climactic Battle of World War II" by Stephen Ambrose. Copyright © 1994 by Ambrose-Tubbs, Inc., by Simon & Schuster, Inc. Reprinted with the permission of Simon & Schuster LLC. All rights reserved, pp. 25-26.
2. Ibid., p. 195.
3. Ibid., p. 314.
4. Ibid., p. 258.
5. Ibid., p. 582.

Chapter 12: Angry Seas (written in part at St. George, 11/5/01, in part at home 12/17/01, 1/12/02, and 1/15/02)

1. Walter Weckler, quoted in PAX Proverbs, (www.dailyinbox.com).

Chapter 13: Seasick (written at Lake Burton, 4/13/01, 3:00 p.m., Good Friday)

1. John Masefield, *Sea-Fever*, reprinted in *Moods of the Sea*, (Annapolis, Maryland: Naval Institute Press, 1981) p. 65.

Chapter 14: Salvage after the Storm (written in the beach room, 5/12/00, 1:30 p.m.)

1. Information about Saffir-Simson Damage Potential Scale found on (http://www .weather.com/breaking_weather/encyclopedia/charts/tropi cal/ss_scale.html)

PART FOUR: GOING ASHORE

Chapter 15: Sound of the Soul (written in the beach room, 7/31/00, 10:54 p.m.)

1. Henry Wadsworth Longfellow, *The Sound of the Sea*, Public Domain.
2. Longfellow, Public Domain.

Chapter 16: A Walk along the Beach (written in the beach room, 7/12/02, 7:52 a.m.)

Chapter 17: Message in a Bottle (written in the beach room, 11/20/00, 9:15 a.m.)

1. Robert Hendrickson, *The Ocean Almanac*, (New York: Doubleday, 1984), pp. 377–78.
2. Ibid., pp. 377–78.
3. Ibid., p. 378.
4. Ibid.
5. Ibid.

Chapter 18: God's Sandcastle (written at Huntington Beach, South Carolina, 8/16/00, 3:58 p.m.)

1. Arthur Clarke, in *The Call of the Sea*, (Great Britain: Exley Publications Ltd., 1999, and New York: Exley Publications LLC, 1999) p. 32.
2. John C. Kricher, *A Peterson First Guide to Seashores*, Copyright © 1992 by John Kricher. Reprinted by permission of Houghton Mifflin Company. All rights reserved, p. 88.
3. Ibid., p. 116.

Chapter 19: Sea Turtle Truths (written at the river, 4/16/00, 4:40 p.m.)

1. SEA TURTLES (http://www.seaworld.org/Sea_Turtle)
2. Ibid.

Chapter 20: Angels of the Sea (written at Lake Burton, 5/29/00, 3:50 a.m.; amended in Ireland, 6/17/00, 10:15 p.m.)

1. Sean Mannion, *Fungie: Ireland's Friendly Dolphin*, (Dingle Co., Kerry, Ireland: Brandon Book Publishers, 1991).
2. Internet Source: http://members.home.net/wamulloy/dolphins/answers
3. Ibid.
4. Mannion, p. 16.
5. Ibid., p. 18.
6. Ibid.
7. Ibid., p. 28.
8. Ibid., p. 30
9. Ibid., p. 122.

Chapter 21: The Lonely Painter and the Sea (written in the beach room, 9/26/02, 12:15 p.m. (This chapter is dedicated to my aspiring painter sister-in-law, Libby Mims, who experienced Vincent's footsteps with me, and who took me to the beach of Saintes Maries de la Mer.)

Many thanks to the Van Gogh Museum in Amsterdam for the historical information about the life of Vincent Van Gogh. This is a wonderful website on which to learn about Van Gogh's life as well as purchase reproductions of his work.

1. Vincent Van Gogh, quoted in the Van Gogh Museum website, Amsterdam, (www.vangoghmuseum.nl/bisrd/top-1-2-2-3-2.html)
2. Vincent Van Gogh in a letter to his brother Theo while in Saintes Maries de la Mer: Marc Guitteny, *Vincent Van Gogh in Provence*, (Monaco: Monaco Press, 2001) p. 21.
3. Ibid., p. 1.
4. The Gypsies and Christianity, Saintes Maries de la Mer in Camargue website, www.saintes-maries.camargue.fr/uk/culturfolk/gitans.html.

Chapter 22: Treasure Chest (written at the river, 2/7/01, 2:30 p.m.)

1. Trent Smalley, *The Hidden Value of a Man*, pp. 133 ff., www.bible.org
2. Michelle Ventor, original source unknown.
3. Quote from the movie, *Forrest Gump*, Paramount Pictures, 1994, used by permission.

Chapter 23: Moondance (written in the beach room, 10/28/00, 11:27 a.m.)

1. Brent Mitchell, in *Fresh Illustrations for Preaching and Teaching* (Baker), from the editors of *Leadership*, found at http://www.preachingtoday.com.

Chapter 24: Vanishing Footprints (written at home, in the beach room, 4/18/00, 4:30 a.m.)

PART FIVE: NOW I SEA EVEN MORE

Chapter 25: The Nautilus Shell (written in the beach room, 3/30/05, 6:47 p.m.)

Chapter 26: I Once Was Blind, But . . . (written in the writing office, 1/9/24, 5:31 p.m.)

1. John Newton, *Amazing Grace, Olney Hymns*, 1779.
2. Steve Turner, *Amazing Grace: The Story of America's Most Beloved Song,* HarperCollins, (2002). pp. 77–79.
3. Jonathan Aitken, *John Newton: From Disgrace to Amazing Grace*, Crossway; Reprint edition (May 31, 2013), p. 227.

PART SIX: BACK IN PORT

1. Alfred Noyes, in *The Call of the Sea*, (Great Britain: Exley Publications Ltd., 1999, and New York: Exley Publications LLC, 1999) p. 72.

Chapter 27: No More Sea (written in the beach room, 9/30/00, 8:40 a.m.)

Chapter 28: Sea for Yourself (written in the beach room, 5/13/00, 8:10 a.m.)

THANKS TO THE CREW

No serious explorer ever embarked on an ambitious voyage without the assistance of a stellar crew. My crew deserves the highest commendation for their incredible support, patience, and wisdom throughout this three-year cruise.

To my heavenly Father—thank you, oh Captain, my Captain! Thanks for who you are and who I am becoming with you at the helm. I gave you this book from day one of the cruise; do with it what you will. Thank you for the privilege of having even been aboard.

My undying love and thanks to the two people who grew me into the Christian sailor I am: my parents, Paul and Janice Mims. Thanks for my joyous childhood and your perpetual love and guidance as I cruised into adulthood and on to write this book. Thank you also for your editing assistance to get this book shipshape.

To all my original feedback crew who reviewed this book as each chapter was written; you all are the finest deck hands I know: Lisa Hockman, Vicki Ofsa, Gena Weaver, Patsy Westall, Leland Free, Jim Johnson, and Willie Oaks. Each of you has brought a different perspective but a unified chorus of encouragement to me. Gena, thank you for giving me your legal pad to write the first words of *Now I Sea* at the beach. I'm so glad you were there when this book was conceived. It broke my heart to lose you, but your legacy lives on in the pages of this book. See you in Heaven, One Heart. My many thanks to Peter Junker, my original editor, colleague, and friend. Peter, you made my "voice" sail from choppy waters into glassy seas! And thank you to my new editor, Rich Cairnes, who keeps my verbiage on course in all my books. It takes a unique person to weather my verbosity with such flying colors. Many thanks to my "Superman with a pen" illustrator Rob Moffitt for creating such a beautiful, new cover. And thank you, Katherine Lloyd, for making this ship's interior as cozy as a boat with cushions.

This book wouldn't be in your hands right now were it not for the love, prayers, and support from my family members near and far. Thank you to my church family at Dunwoody Baptist Church in Dunwoody, Georgia. And thank you to my long-distance church family at Calvary Chapel Chino Hills. Pastor Jack, I'm so very grateful for your ministry that helps to keep me on course with hopeful horizons and full sails all the way. Thank you for prompting me to update *Now I Sea* for such a time as this. *Soli Deo Gloria.*

Finally, thanks to my first mate Casey and yeoman Alex. Thank you for your love and patience with me through smooth sailing and rough seas. Thank you for the freedom to run the gunnels in writing this book, for my travels at home and abroad, and my time away at the keyboard.

Aye, 'tis a fine crew indeed!

ABOUT THE AUTHOR

Jenny L. Cote is an award-winning author and speaker who developed an early passion for God, history, and young people. She beautifully blends these three passions in her two fantasy fiction series, *The Amazing Tales of Max and Liz®* and *Epic Order of the Seven®*. Likened to C. S. Lewis by readers and book reviewers alike, she speaks on creative writing to schools, universities, and conferences around the world. Jenny has a passion for making history fun for kids of all ages, instilling in them a desire to discover their part in HIStory. Her love for research has taken her to most Revolutionary sites in the U.S., to London (with unprecedented access to Handel House Museum to write in Handel's composing room), Oxford (to stay in the home of C. S. Lewis, 'the Kilns', and interview Lewis' secretary, Walter Hooper, at the Inklings' famed The Eagle and Child Pub), Paris, Normandy, Rome, Israel, and Egypt. She partnered with the National Park Service to create Epic Patriot Camp, a summer writing camp at Revolutionary parks to excite kids about history, research, and writing. Jenny's books are available online and in stores around the world, as well as in e-book and audio formats. Jenny has been featured by FOX NEWS on Fox & Friends and local Fox Affiliates, as well as numerous Op-Ed pieces on FoxNews.com. She has also been interviewed by nationally syndicated radio and print media, as well as international publications. Jenny holds two marketing degrees from the University of Georgia and Georgia State University. A Virginia native, Jenny now lives with her family in Roswell, Georgia. Official website: www.epicorderoftheseven.com.

JENNY L. COTE'S HISTORICAL FICTION SERIES

Start listening at audible.com

Learn more at www.epicorderoftheseven.com.

SAME CHARACTERS, TWO AWARD-WINNING SERIES

The adventure begins with the two-book prequel series: *The Amazing Tales of Max & Liz®*, where the Maker begins building His team of animals to be His envoys through pivotal points of history. Max, Liz, Kate, and Al launch the adventure in book one, *The Ark, the Reed, and the Fire Cloud,* and are joined by their British mouse friend, Nigel, in book two, *The Dreamer, the Schemer, and the Robe.* With book three, *The Prophet, the Shepherd, & the Star,* the team of seven animals is finally complete, and known forevermore as the Order of the Seven in the *Epic Order of the Seven®* series. Working behind the scenes in the lives of Jesus, the Disciples, Paul and the early church, the team will pass through Biblical and world history up to modern times with Patrick Henry, Lafayette, and the Revolutionary War, and C.S. Lewis and World War II.

The Epic Revolutionary Saga

The Voice, the Revolution, and the Key: 1743–75, the founders as kids, events leading up to the eve of Revolution.

The Declaration, the Sword, and the Spy: 1775–76, Lexington and Concord, Bunker Hill, siege of Boston through the Declaration of Independence.

The Marquis, the Escape, and the Fox: 1776–77, the Battle of New York, Trenton, Princeton, escape of the Marquis de Lafayette from France, and France's secret aid to America.

More titles to follow to complete the entire story of the American Revolution and the founding of the United States of America.

SCHEDULE JENNY L. COTE TO SPEAK TO YOUR GROUP

Award-winning author Jenny L. Cote opens the world of creative writing and history for students of all ages and reading levels through fun, highly interactive workshops. Jenny has appeared to thousands of students at homeschool groups and conferences, lower, middle, and high schools, writing conferences, churches, book clubs, historical groups, and universities in the U.S. and abroad. Jenny's workshops correspond to her specific books, showing students exactly how she crafts her books, from research to character development to imagery. It gives students real hands-on tools used by an author, with a behind-the-scenes look at how a book comes together. Surprising grand entrances, fun props, and humorous questions keep students engaged from the first minute, with smiles and hands raised to be chosen to do the next fun thing!

Learn more at www.epicorderoftheseven.com.

Made in United States
Troutdale, OR
08/22/2024

22224267R00148